TINA HOUSER'S
FASCINATING PRESCHOOLERS

WITH KELLEY HOUSER

Warner Press, Inc.
Warner Press and "Warner Press" logo are trademarks of Warner Press, Inc.

Fascinating Preschoolers
Written by Tina Houser with Kelley Houser

©2017 Warner Press, Inc.

Requests for information should be sent to:
Warner Press Inc
2902 Enterprise Dr
P.O. Box 2499
Anderson, IN 46013
www.warnerpress.org

Editors: Karen Rhodes, Robin Fogle
Creative Director: Curtis D. Corzine
Layout: Katie Miller

ISBN: 978-1-59317-645-8
This book is also available in e-book format
Printed in USA

BIG TIME THANK YOU!

This book has been a delight to put together, mainly because I find an amazing amount of joy when I have the opportunity to fascinate preschoolers. I love their wide eyes. I love how they wait for you to do the unexpected. I love their unconditional hugs. I love when they are amazed by the stories of God's faithful people.

Let me pause for a few moments and express some BIG TIME THANK YOUS. Thank you to the team at Warner Press, especially Karen Rhodes, who was so understanding about a missed deadline. I had some major health issues surface right when the files were due, and they graciously took the pressure off to "get 'er done."

Thank you to all the preschoolers in my life who constantly inspire me to figure out something new they'll be fascinated by. Bowen and Kendall (my 7-year-old grandtwins) have now moved beyond the preschool years, but it's only due to the challenge of staying one step ahead of them that the activities in this book came to be. And now their little sister, Lucy, has entered the world, and I'm so pumped about getting the opportunity to fascinate her also. I love the preschoolers I get to love on at our church. Their smiles and hugs are a constant reward for preparing fascinating activities. Some of them are pictured in this book: Alex Oswald, McKenna Graf, Olivia Graf, and Emma Graf. They were amazing at the photo shoot! And, to those preschoolers I don't even know—the ones I see when I'm shopping or at the park—thank you for accepting my smile. I pray that someone fascinates your own personal relationship with God.

I never want it to go unsaid that I am forever grateful for the support of my husband, Ray, and son, Jarad. They always encourage me to stretch much further than I think is possible. When you have wind in your sails, like Ray and Jarad provide, you don't hesitate to shoot for the stars. To say I love them and appreciate them is far too little.

The thanks I want to express to my lovely, talented daughter-in-law, Kelley, is huge…gargantuan…humongous! Kelley's really the one who has enlightened me on how to fascinate preschoolers. I continually learn from watching how she communicates with the littlest ones. She's a master! Many of the ideas in this book were inspired by Kelley or tweaked from projects we have worked on together. Thank You, Lord, for the gift of such a beautiful godly woman who blesses our entire family.

Thank You, Lord, for giving me opportunities to ignite others to minister to and with preschoolers. I am so blessed to serve You and want to do that with every ounce of energy and enthusiasm You give me. I'm grateful to be able to capture the ideas You put in my brain and use them to touch the lives of children I will never meet this side of heaven. You are my good, good Father.

In His incredible joy, *Tina!*

TABLE OF CONTENTS

UNDERSTANDING PRESCHOOLERS

FASCINATING ACTIVITIES

FASCINATING FOOD

FASCINATING PAINTING

FASCINATING SCIENCE

FASCINATING VOCABULARY

FASCINATING SEQUENCING RELAYS

EMBRACING FASCINATION

A preschooler's existence is all about learning what their world is like. This includes their body, their family, the community, and anything else that happens across their path. The things that we take for granted…things that are commonplace…may never have been experienced by a preschooler. This is something new! They're seeing it for the first time, and it's *FASCINATING!* It doesn't mean that it's a new technology, which fascinates adults more. It simply means that it's new to them.

Embrace their fascination. They're trying to do something on their own and it's fascinating. Yes, how to change the stations on the radio is fascinating to a preschooler. Yes, getting peanut butter on a piece of bread is fascinating to a preschooler. Yes, sitting on the top of the dryer and pulling wet clothes out of the washing machine is fascinating to a preschooler. How ordinary and mundane to adults, but how fascinating to preschoolers.

Preschoolers are notorious for asking questions. They want to find out more about what they're seeing and experiencing for the first time. You can collect all kinds of figures about the number of questions a preschooler asks each day (anywhere between 200 and 800!). If you're conservative and go with the lowest number on that scale, my goodness, that's still a lot of questions! The more you fascinate kids, though, the more questions they're going to ask, so get ready. Their questions are a super-valuable tool for retaining information from their fascinating experience. Don't discount those questions.

Preschoolers learn through experiences and not simply listening to words. Experiences build their vocabulary exponentially. Every new word also has new ways of describing it, which means more vocabulary. Our goal is not to cram knowledge into kids, but to *FASCINATE* them with the wonders of the world God created. Direct them to new experiences, and don't be satisfied to keep repeating the same ones. It takes a little extra work to stay out of a rut. But, it makes teaching these little ones so much more interesting when you're there, and they discover something for the very first time.

So, what fascinates a preschooler? Just about anything—anything they've not seen before—anything they've not done before. Did you know that fascination has a sound? It's a squeal of delight. It's an, "Oh my goodness!" It's talking fast and saying the same thing over and over, because they don't know what to ask first. It's giggles. It's hearing, "Do that again!" because once just isn't enough. The sounds of fascination make my heart soar! They are my reward and my motivation when I'm preparing.

Embrace fascination. Make it the banner that flies over your ministry to preschoolers. Create experiences that will fascinate them with the Word of God and with their Creator, Savior, and Lord. If this is the time when their brains are taking in more information than at any other time in their lives, then we need to take advantage of that by introducing them to a foundation of faith in the One True God. Don't make their learning just about numbers and letters, but help them learn about the love letter God has written to each of us.

Speak the language of fascination and you will find great satisfaction and joy.

Tinsley and Maelyn Gardner sat in front of the oven door and watched their peanut butter muffins bake for 30 minutes. Why? Because they were fascinated!

PRESCHOOL PHYSICAL DEVELOPMENT

Preschoolers go through developmental stages so quickly! The child you have this week most likely will not have the same capabilities next week. Vocabulary is growing by close to 100 words a month. Social skills are taking hold. And, their physical development changes almost daily. The child who was totally unable to stand on one foot last Sunday can now rival a flamingo this Sunday.

Parents, teachers, and children's ministry leaders are all on the same team. They all are interested in the whole child and seeing each one develop in a well-rounded manner. So, it's wise to incorporate age-appropriate activities that will exercise the specific developmental stage of the preschoolers you teach.

Let's look at some physical things they are learning to do and how we can include those activities in our biblical teaching.

Sweeping
Preschoolers are learning the sweeping motion.
- Practice with a small broom to actually clean up.
- Sweep a ping-pong ball into the correct bucket—one with a smile or one with a frown—to respond to a situation.
- Put animal stickers on milk jug caps. Give the kids dustpans and hand brooms (from the dollar store) to gather up the animals to put on the ark.

Balancing
From balancing their entire body to balancing something in a spoon, balancing is a big part of physical development.
- Walk across balance beams to retrieve something to do with your lesson.
- Write questions on cardboard pancakes. Challenge the kids to carry one across the room on a pancake turner. When they reach the wall, they can respond to the question.
- Walk across inflatable pool mattresses (end to end) when telling the story of Jesus walking on the water.
- Balance a beanbag on your head and walk to the "hillside" where Jesus is talking. Beanbags are so flexible and much easier to keep on your head than a book—a great place to begin.

Jumping

- Jump in front of a full-length mirror. Kids love to see themselves jump, and they are not familiar with what they look like from head to toe.

- Jump between two boards as if jumping across the river/sea. Then, move the boards a little bit further apart. Talk about the Israelites crossing the Jordan River or the Red Sea. The river is wide!

Using Tools

- Hammers are fascinating to preschoolers. When Jesus was a boy, He learned how to work with wood by practicing at Joseph's feet. Have nails already started in wood, and let the kids pound to their hearts' content.

- Use a large spike and big piece of wood to practice hammering when talking about Jesus being nailed to the cross. Listen to the sound.

Digging

- Mix some brown M&Ms in a bucket of potting soil. The kids can use spoons or toy claw gardening tools to find the M&Ms. We must decide what is good and what is bad…what are good choices and what are bad choices. They may look alike, and we need to separate the good and bad choices.

- Plant seeds so kids can watch a plant grow. Isn't God amazing!

Pinching

They are learning to bring their fingers to their thumb in order to cause the pinching motion.
- Use appetizer tongs to pick up Styrofoam packing peanuts. Gather manna or sheep.

- Fold a paper plate in half; then decorate it like a face. Kids can pinch the plate together to use as a puppet. Normally shy children will respond to questions and carry on conversations when they have a puppet.

- Use grabbers—long sticks with an animal head on the end—to move objects from one place to another.

Pouring

Preschoolers love to pour!
- Pass several ping-pong balls from cup to cup around a circle while music plays. When the music stops, the kids with a ball in their cup will say the memory verse together.

- A child will carry a half-cup of water, while walking on his knees, to someone at the end of the room. That person will have his/her bare feet in a pan. The child will pour his water on the person's feet and say, "Jesus washed their feet." Or, this could go along with the woman kneeling to pour perfume on Jesus' feet.

Tossing/Throwing

- The kids can take turns tossing beanbags into a tub or inflatable pool ring. Each time a beanbag goes in, the teacher will yell out another disciple's name: "Peter was in the boat!" Then, the kids will echo this back before the next person tosses. When the thirteenth beanbag goes in, yell, "Jesus joined them in the boat!"

- Cut pool noodles into 18" lengths. The leader will hold a hulahoop, and the kids will toss their pool noodles through the hoop. Use this with the story of David and Jonathan—with the pool noodle representing the arrows that Jonathan is shooting as a message to David. When a noodle goes through the hoop, the child should shout, "Go farther!"

Oh my, there are a zillion more skills—bouncing, rolling, climbing, catching! Think about how you can incorporate the natural physical development stages into your next lesson. Your kids will be more engaged and will have one more opportunity to hone those skills.

THIS IS MY SPACE

Defining individual space boundaries for preschoolers

Space is an abstract concept, and preschoolers don't exactly know what "space" means. You're talking to yourself when you say, "Spread out so you've got some room!" They're not sure what "spread out" means. There are times when it's okay to have these little ones huddled together, sitting up against one another, or even on top of one another. During free playtime, they wander in and out of one another's spaces, and it's part of the flow. But, many times you will find, it lends itself to order and fewer discipline problems when each child is just a little out of reach of the next child. We can help them by giving them tangible ways to define their individual spaces.

Why should we consider identifying a preschooler's space? I'm glad you asked! Preschoolers are developing their social skills and are easily distracted by one another. When kids are in close proximity, the leader spends as much—if not more—time reconfiguring kids and vying for their attention than in leading the actual activity. These little ones are also learning about boundaries. Before they understand the abstract perspective, they need to experience the concrete aspect of having physical boundaries. (For many kids, especially those with focus issues, it takes years to go from having a physical boundary to understanding the invisible.)

Preschoolers are beginning to identify shapes, the first one being the circle. You can put a circle in front of them, and they can call it by name. They will start seeing things in their environment that resemble a circle and pointing those out. They may even be able to draw a circle with a crayon. But transferring that to sitting in a circle goes from concrete to abstract and things fall apart QUICKLY! You could take each child by the shoulders and move them into position, or you could provide a way to identify their particular spot. The second way is quicker, smoother, and puts the responsibility in the child's hands rather than the leader's.

"Circle time" is a common preschool designation. One of the easiest ways to accomplish this is with a rug that has the positions already printed on it, although many times the spaces are awfully close together. A quick Internet search will provide you with plenty of rug options that are theme-related and educational, while providing the indicated spaces for kids. Other things that accomplish the same thing as a rug, but give the leader more flexibility in adjusting the space for each child are:

- **CARPET SQUARES** These remnants come with the edges professionally bound and can be purchased for as little as one dollar from carpet stores. You can choose colors that go with the theme of your room. They're cushy and can be placed on the floor in any configuration.

- **PLACEMATS** The fun thing about using placemats to define personal spaces is that you can make them seasonal or related to a holiday. You can also get them in cut-out figures rather than the traditional rectangle, like giant leaf placemats for fall or flower placemats in the spring.

- **HULA HOOPS** Purchase the small hula hoops and lay them on the floor. They don't have to be spread out, but can bump up against one another. Each kid sits inside his own hula hoop, which provides ample room and obvious boundaries.

- **PILLOWS** The leader calls a name, the child runs to pick up a pillow, and sits where the leader was standing. The leader moves to the next space and continues calling names and doing the same thing. Developmentally, this helps preschoolers envision the circle being created.

Many preschool rooms do not utilize chairs, and the kids sit on the floor for most activities. For the child who just has a lot of energy and can't sit still for two seconds, even with the help of one of the space indicators we just mentioned, the answer may be as simple as a chair. A chair has a different quality to it that is more defined and confined. We had a boy (who we'll call George for now) who constantly moved through the room at a half-run, and seemed to intentionally like to cause chaos…and he loved to be chased. One day I asked him, "George, would you like your own chair?" We brought a chair into the classroom, and he was told that he could sit in it whenever he wanted to. It was only for him. We gave him guidelines for how it was to be moved for different activities. There was an immediate difference—night and day. He began participating appropriately and enjoying the time together much more. All because of a chair! We figured out how to connect him with his space boundaries.

This is going to sound harsh and maybe questionable to some of you, but another way we've actually delightfully created space boundaries for preschoolers is by providing a large, open plastic tub. It's along the back wall and is designated for specific children. When we introduced the tub, it was specifically for one child (who we'll call Henry). Interestingly enough, we've never had any of the other children ask to use the tub, and they understand that this is Henry's special place. What a wonderful lesson in helping kids accept each other's differences! When Henry is getting disruptive, a leader will remind him gently about his opportunity to utilize the tub, but after a few weeks of having it available, he started self-regulating and now goes on his own to the tub when he feels the anxiety build. That's a huge step developmentally!

The tub is a very well-received tool by our special needs kids. They are often overwhelmed when there are additional kids in attendance and the "feel" of the room is a little different. Climbing into the tub provides not only a definition on the floor, but also on the sides. Many experts in autism indicate that having the feeling of being wrapped (walls of the tub) actually has a calming effect on the child. To keep the tub connected to the class, we usually tape a picture that goes along with the lesson for that day to an inside wall.

As you can see, defining spaces for preschoolers becomes an individual task—finding just the right space boundaries that fit each child. There are blanket methods that most kids will respond to, like the placemats and carpet squares, but for the ones that these don't satisfy, you need to explore other options. Before we can teach kids anything about our wonderful God and His Word, we have to create a space that fits their needs and will provide the best possible learning environment for each one.

MONDAY STORIES

Early childhood/preschool ministry is extremely important for laying a spiritual foundation in little ones, but we often think that true spiritual growth can't really start happening until the grade school years. Even if staff people comprehend the concept, the laypeople in the church have definitely not wrapped their minds around the impact that pouring into the lives of preschoolers can have on the church and on eternity. So, how do we go from the bulk of the church (and many volunteers) thinking that preschool ministry is basically corralling the kids while services and programs take place for older kids and adults…to grasping how critical it is to begin their lifelong journey with Christ as Savior and Lord from the day these little ones take their first breath?

There are several strategies for approaching the slow and steady mindset shift, but right now I want to share with you about one—Monday Stories. In order for people to believe that preschool ministry is worth resources, time, training, and commitment, they have to be educated that something is happening. Even though they're not in the rooms telling stories, playing games, changing diapers, dishing up Cheerios, or singing songs, they need to connect with what's taking place in those rooms. That's where Monday Stories come in.

What's a Monday Story?

It's the story you start telling each Monday about one particular positive thing that happened on Sunday when you were with the kids. And you keep telling that story over and over and over again throughout the week, anytime you get a new audience. You post it on Facebook (your page and the church's page). You talk about it with the parents of those kids. You mention it when you're in life group with other adults and you're sharing how God is on the move. Excitedly, you bring it up when you're out to lunch with friends and when you're doing chores around the church. Anyone who will engage you in conversation, for any reason, is a candidate for hearing your Monday Story.

What happened on Sunday that was evidence God is working in the life of a preschooler? In order to share a Monday Story, you need to personally raise your antennae and open your eyes. You need to be more aware of what's happening in their lives. Monday Stories don't have to be earth-shaking, life-changing events. They simply need to be joy moments when you notice little ones taking steps toward Jesus.

What happens when you make sharing Monday Stories a habit? Lots!

1. It changes you. You start looking at the kids you lead with anticipation for how their hearts and minds are being molded to reach for God. Things that you normally wouldn't notice now become something you hold on to. As you weekly see results—no matter how small—it increases the value you put on preparing and leading. You don't need someone else thanking you for serving or encouraging you, because the Monday Story you come away with is the boost you need and God's way of saying, "Well done, my good and faithful servant."

2. It's contagious. A fellow children's pastor shared with me that she had decided to implement Monday Stories as part of her week. Repeatedly, she shared the tidbit of how God was moving among the preschoolers when it was her turn to share in the church staff meetings. Instead of going through the bullet points of the agenda, a refreshing positive tone was set for each meeting. The youth pastor saw the impact it was having and adopted the practice in respect to the youth. Anyone can share Monday Stories!

3. It educates. Monday Stories aren't a once-a-year occurrence. Each week you're pointing out the growth you're noticing. Those people who are hearing the stories can't help but realize that preschoolers are capable of growing in remarkably profound spiritual ways. It's one of the best ways to dispel the notion that preschool ministry is only babysitting.

4. Monday Stories draw people into preschool ministry. People want to be involved where things are happening and where they know they can make a difference. One story won't do it. But when you consistently share a variety of things about different kids, recruiting is easier. When people have heard about the great experiences that are taking place—how kids are both enjoying and growing spiritually, and team members are leading them through steps of spiritual growth—they're willing to step in where it's obvious God is working.

5. Monday Stories have a snowball effect of making it easier for parishioners to invite guests with preschoolers. They can insure the families they're inviting that their children will have a great experience, because they've heard the stories of what's happening in that ministry.

Monday Stories don't cost a thing, but they have a huge impact! Open your eyes, ears, and heart this coming Sunday, so you'll be ready on Monday to start elevating preschool ministry in the eyes of those who aren't sure how the little ones are growing closer to God with each experience.

A Few Monday Stories

During our worship time, one 6-year-old boy always closes his eyes anytime we sing "Good, Good Father." He's done that since the day we introduced it. Today, as the song began, there were boys on each side of him who were being somewhat distracting. He quietly moved to the side of the room where he closed his eyes and continued to worship. That said a lot about what was important to him at that moment, and he wasn't going to give it up. I love to see these moments of spiritual growth…and I also love that the other leaders are recognizing it too.

A parent sent me a short video of her youngest daughter (who is in the toddler nursery) singing, "Tell the world that Jesus lives!" We had a 7-year-old and two 6-year-olds lead our worship in kids' church today. It was the first time for all three, and they introduced two new songs. Killed it! I just stepped back and basically said, "Let 'er rip, tater chip!" I'm sure God was enjoying the celebration, and it was amazing to watch how the three kids took ownership in what they were doing. This was serious stuff to them—my heart was full.

A sister and brother put up a lemonade stand, complete with fruit kabobs, cake pops, and cookies they had worked on for days. It was one of the most successful lemonade stands I'd ever heard of, with each of the kids making over $36. After separating the coins into two identical piles, and without prompting from any adult, their first question was, "Can you help us figure out how much to give to the church?" They brought their sandwich bags of coins to place their first tithe in the offering plate that next Sunday.

UNDERSTANDING PRESCHOOLERS
SLOW DOWN!

Around the year I was in third-grade, my family started taking an annual summer vacation to Daytona Beach, Florida, from our home in southern Indiana. The station wagon that faithfully carried us there was one that had the bench seat that looked out the back window, so my brother, sister, and I sat and watched the road where we HAD been and waved at truckers behind us (and tried to get them to sound their air horns). As the sun dropped past the horizon, that seat was flattened to make a bed where three little kids curled up in their sleeping bags to watch the stars out that same back window.

It was a 14-hour drive, and my dad's idea of getting there was to make it in 14 hours, which meant very few breaks along the way. The only time we stopped was when the station wagon needed fuel. Bathroom visits had to be made in the time it took him to put the nozzle in the car and make his payment. Everyone was expected to be back in the car when he returned with the receipt. Any food we wanted was in the cooler or grocery sack brought from home.

Dad was on a mission! Point A was home and Point B was the hotel in Florida. Nothing in between those points was of interest to him. The pedal was to the metal, his eyes were straight forward, and his ears were listening to Mom as she navigated. Nothing deterred Dad from obtaining his goal. He had a plan and no one was going to mess with it. It wasn't until after I got married that I realized there are really interesting historical markers along the roads that make a great little place to stop and stretch, or that you can actually pull off at an exit…just to get a drink!

Unfortunately, many of us are like my dad when it comes to teaching preschoolers. We've read our lesson plan, gathered all the supplies, and maybe even cut out a bunch of pieces of construction paper that the kids will put together in 2 minutes flat and then not really look like what we intended. We've put effort into preparing and nothing is going to get in our way…not even these little ones whose main interest lies in exploring their world.

Preschoolers notoriously go off on little side trips. To a preschooler a simple walk down the hall is successful if it includes talking about the five pictures of kids from the church that hang on the wall, wondering where a door leads, and just wanting to stop and rest halfway. But that's not what we have in mind. The clock is ticking and we've got to get through all these awesome activities.

Part of being an effective preschool teacher is respecting that these little people haven't experienced everything you take for granted and are still learning about the simplest of things. We've got to give them time to process all the random and somewhat insignificant things we look right past. Give them time to explore this world that God brought them into.

Slow down! This isn't about you. It's about them. It's not about getting from Point A to Point B. It's about everything that comes between Point A and Point B. It's not about getting to every activity in the lesson plan. It's about pointing the preschoolers in your care to Jesus in every single thing you do and say. So, take a deep breath. Don't get frantic when time seems to be slipping away, and you've not gotten as far as you had planned in your lesson.

When it's a pretty day and you take your preschoolers out to sit under a tree to hear the story of Zacchaeus, be prepared to give a lot more time than it actually takes to tell the story. First of all, the walk from the classroom to the storytelling tree holds lots of magical moments. There are rocks to be picked up, bugs to watch, things to point out that are across the street, in the air, or around the corner of the building. If it bothers you to not get through the lesson plan, then just plan extra "discovery" time into the plan that happens in transit. Put transition time on your to-do list/lesson plan, then it won't catch you off guard or feel like it's robbing you. During this slowed down discovery time, you can even initiate some of the discovery and join right in the excitement over new things.

If you're reading a new book—one that the kids have not yet seen or heard—make sure everyone can see the pictures. Stop. Don't even think about turning that page! Pause and ask questions. "Can you find the…?" "Where do you think the man is going?" "Why is the man sitting in the tree?" Give them time to point out what they notice in the pictures. Their picture smart multiple intelligence is in high gear right now. You and I, old and young—we all think in pictures, but preschoolers are building a full vocabulary by what they experience visually. When all the questions have been answered, then, and only then, ask the kids, "Is it time to turn the page?" to which you'll get a resounding, "Yes!" They won't be constantly trying to turn the page back because they weren't finished yet.

I'm an awful lot like my dad—always in high gear and very goal-oriented. I'm not really fond of down time. That's why I have to be extra conscious when I'm leading preschoolers…to get out of my own head and into theirs. I could walk right past all the discoveries still left to be made. I think that's why I love working with preschoolers so much. They slow me down. They point out the things I've missed. They bother to ask the questions I've not even considered asking.

One of my favorite children's movies is *Finding Nemo*. And, although I have too many "favorite" parts of that movie to list, one character I love is the whale. I love that whale because of the way he talks…slowly… very, very slowly. So, say it along with me in "whale talk", S-L-O-W D-O-W-N! Commit to embracing this new mindset when you welcome your preschoolers this next week. Think, "I'm going to point them to Jesus…in everything we do…on a preschooler's time schedule…no matter how long it takes!"

WHAT'S MORE IMPORTANT?

When we think about brain development, we tend to think about intelligence and knowledge—knowing stuff. But, is the fact that preschoolers know their letters, numbers, and colors by age four really the most important thing for them to be learning? Various studies have shown that mastering executive function skills contributes much more to the foundation that will prepare preschoolers for school and life beyond the preschool years.

What are executive function skills? Although the term sounds very technical and proper, it's really *FASCINATING* to think about, and extraordinarily important for these little people to be grasping. Executive function breaks down into four general skills, and incorporating these into ministering to preschoolers is a huge way to partner with parents and teachers. Knowledgably addressing each of these executive function skills invites kids to succeed! It helps build who they are more than what they know.

So let's take a look at these four executive function skills.

Attention Focus

This is where you help children learn how to focus their attention, how to sustain it, and then how to transition to another activity. Preschoolers are notorious for being distracted. It's like herding cats! So much of what they learn will depend on them being able to focus.

A great goal for young preschoolers is to successfully get them to sustain their focus for 3-5 minutes. You, as the leader, cannot get them to do this unless you have a plan. If you walk into your classroom without a plan, you're going to be frustrated because the kids will not stay on task. Preschool leaders, more than anyone, need to have a clear and concise lesson plan.

The smaller you can make your groups, the easier it is to keep kids focused. That's because they can see what's being displayed, they have more opportunities to participate individually, and they feel like they have their leader's attention. So, if you have helpers in your room, divide the kids into groups and duplicate the activities under the leadership of your helpers.

Sustain preschoolers' focus by keeping them engaged. Preschoolers are not engaged by talk. They want action. They want *FASCINATION!* On those occasions when you want to have "serious talk", pull chairs into a semi-circle. (That's the only time my kids sit in chairs; otherwise, they're on the floor or standing around the table.) The chairs actually become a change in environment and contribute to holding their attention. If you're presenting a story, don't just read it from a book. You need pictures, objects they can feel, phrases and words they need to listen for, or use a unique storytelling technique, like black light stories, costumed characters, or puppets. (You can find lots of storytelling techniques in my book, *Going Live in 3…2…1!*)

Where preschool teachers most often lose kids' attention is during transitions—moving from music to craft, or from an object lesson to a game, story to prayer time, or moving from one room to another. When you fail to plan your transitions, then you're inviting the kids to lose focus. You'll spend as much time trying to get their attention once again as you do in an actual activity. Be the master of transitions by:

- Having all your supplies in place before the first child arrives.

- Preparing craft kit bags, where everything a child needs for a craft is in a ziplock bag.

- Providing a sample of a completed craft project.

- Marking starting lines for games on the floor with masking tape (prior to class time).

- Reviewing scriptures, especially to music, as you walk down the hallway.

- Giving all the directions for the next activity before moving to that area.

Don't give away any of the precious time you have with your preschoolers by not having your transitions planned. That's time you could turn their eyes toward God and His Word.

Impulse Control

Impulse control is the ability to not always do or say the first thing that comes to mind. Preschoolers are definitely working on this skill, but need lots of guidance and tools.

One tool is for YOU to learn how to make statements. You can inadvertently welcome a lack of impulse control by the way you ask a question when all you really want to do is make a statement. In one particular instance I asked a question, rather than made a statement: "Has anyone ever gotten a splinter?" This question invited every child to tell his or her splinter story, resulting in chaos. I should've said, "Grab your big toe if you've ever had a splinter." This statement (rather than the question) gives them an action to use as their response. Each child would be engaged without going off in ten different story directions.

Figure out ways kids will know when it is appropriate to respond, instead of just yelling out their answer. You can ring a counter bell or give a hand signal when you're ready for kids to raise their hands. Or, honk a horn when they can all yell out their answers at one time. Preface your question with: "When I ask the question, if you know the answer, then grab your elbow." And, one of the best ways to help kids with impulse control is to randomly draw their names for the opportunity to respond. You can do this as simply as writing all their names on craft sticks and putting them in a container. Make sure they see that all sticks are drawn out before anyone gets a second turn. This reinforces their impulse control and helps them work through the sometimes difficult preschool fairness issues.

Working Memory

Working memory is the ability to hold and use multiple thoughts in your mind. Rather than you giving the kids one instruction and waiting for that to be completed before moving on, give them several directions at once. Games are great for this!

Sequencing relays are wonderful for this. You give the kids three or four stations to visit. At each station they must use a prop and repeat a phrase that goes along with that prop. These stations represent parts of the story, so they are working with multiple thoughts at one time in order to put the story together.

Another great game for working memory is using obstacle courses. Always demonstrate exactly what you want the kids to do—remember they do not engage through talk, so show them. Your obstacle course may consist of zigzagging through traffic cones, walking on a balance beam, and then jumping through a hula hoop. But don't just tell them that; do it! Their working memory will then have to re-enact the steps they saw you do.

You can exercise working memory as you put crafts together or when you're making snacks that go along with the story. Encourage the kids to explain the steps of making the snack and how it relates to the story. (See my book *More Than Cookies and Punch* for snack ideas.)

Planning

The fourth executive function skill that you can help preschoolers with is learning to plan and carry out a sequence of actions in order to reach a goal or solve a problem, adjusting those plans along the way as needed.

One of the best ways I can think of to do this in the context of children's ministry is to propose that the kids come up with a plan for a service project. They plan by answering questions like:

• What would you like to do?

• What will we have to get ready so we can do it?

• When will we do it?

• Whose help will we need?

You'll be amazed at what you'll notice as your preschoolers plan their service projects. Gifts of leadership will become obvious. Take note of those natural leaders and pour into them. They WILL become leaders, because that's the way God has wired them. How we train them will determine if they lead people toward God or away from Him.

What's really cool about the four executive function skills…

• Attention Focus

• Impulse Control

• Working Memory

• Planning

…is that they are influenced by nurture, experience, and interaction. It's not about obedience or getting kids to sit still. It's about partnering with their overall development in the best possible way! It provides ways to build relationships with kids, rather than have them memorizing facts, colors, numbers, and letters. As these four executive function skills develop, you'll find that discipline issues are minimized and you enjoy teaching even more.

A NEW T-SHIRT

Romans 5:6 (ICB)

Christ died for us while we were still weak. We were living against God, but at the right time, Christ died for us.

Needed:

- Black construction paper
- Large T-shirt, any color
- Large white T-shirt
- Tape

Salvation is a difficult concept to grasp, but we need to start laying the foundation at an early age. Providing many different visuals helps kids put the pieces together and understand what Jesus actually did.

- Choose two children to help with this activity. Place a large T-shirt (any color) over one child's regular clothes; then, place a large white T-shirt over the other child's clothes.

- **Beforehand**, cut out pieces of black construction paper that will represent sin. The shape of the black paper should look like a blotch. With every sin discussed, the leader will tape a black blotch to the child's any-colored shirt.

Address the child who has on the colored T-shirt.

- *Let's pretend this child's name is Jimmy. Jimmy is totally bummed today. His week was really rough. It seemed that he made really poor choices everywhere he went.*

- *On Monday, Jimmy got angry at the playground and said some things to this kid that were really mean.* (Attach a sin-blotch to the child.)

- *On Tuesday, Jimmy's parents asked him to put away his toy trucks that were in the hallway and he just ignored them. So, when Mom got up in the middle of the night, she tripped over them and fell into the cabinets. He totally disobeyed his parents.* (Attach a sin-blotch to the child.)

- *On Thursday, Jimmy lied to his preschool teacher. He told her that he hadn't been the helper of the day yet, when he really had been just the week before.* (Attach a sin-blotch to the child.)

- *On Friday, Jimmy got a time-out for being mean to his little sister. But she was such a pest to Jimmy! Still...he really should not have shoved her.* (Attach a sin-blotch to the child.)

- *And then on Saturday, it seemed like Jimmy couldn't do anything right! He may have set a record for the number of times anyone had ever been put in time-out!* (Attach several sin-blotches to the child.)

- *What a week! Jimmy feels covered in the things that he did wrong. These are what we call sin. Have any of you ever felt this way? Have you ever had a day, or a week, when you were always getting into trouble?*

Talking to the child in the white T-shirt.

- *You represent Jesus. You're wearing white, because you're the perfect Son of God. You never once disobeyed God. You never made bad choices and sinned. But when we disobey, we get punished. So, God should punish us for not obeying Him, right?*

- *(Point to kid representing Jesus)*

- *When You (Jesus) died on the cross, you (Jesus) took the punishment for Jimmy's sins.* The child wearing the white T-shirt representing Jesus will remove the stained any-colored T-shirt from the other child and then remove his own white T-shirt. He will then place his white T-shirt on the other child, and put on the T-shirt covered with sin blotches. (Point to the appropriate kids as you speak.)

- *We should be punished for all the things we've done against God. But Jesus says He will take that punishment for us when we ask Him, and when we believe that He is God's Son. Because Jesus took our punishment, our lives are clean, and God gives us a brand new start.*

ANYTHING'S A PUPPET

Needed:

- Googly eyes, all sizes

Some people think you have to have professionally made puppets in order to use them effectively.

NOT AT ALL!

Some people think you have to be a ventriloquist if you're going to use puppets effectively.

NOT AT ALL!

Some people think you have to have a fancy stage with curtains in order to use puppets effectively.

NOPE!

When a puppet appears, preschoolers connect with the puppet. I hate to break this to you, but you no longer exist to the preschoolers. You can talk for the puppet, and they're not paying any attention to your mouth. You can hold the puppet up in front of you, and they don't care that there's not a curtain separating you. And, they most certainly don't care if your puppet is handmade or something you paid $100+ for.

One day I discovered something about puppets. (Actually, I intended to dust the house, but the dust mitt was calling me to do otherwise.) I looked at the brand new dust mitt and I thought, "What would happen if I gave you a face?" I located a set of googly eyes and laid them on the dust mitt. That's all it took! It came to life. It needed no more face…which is a little confusing to me. Why is it that a pair of eyes can somehow make something appear able to talk?

Once the dust mitt surrendered its original duties and now entered the world as a puppet, I realized that there were other similar cleaning rag mitts that would do the same thing. Now I have a family for the original dust mitt puppet—an older, taller brother and a baby sister.

But, it goes further! Find anything, place those eyes on it…and "Voilà!"…you have a puppet. Eyes on a toaster…your toaster can talk. Eyes on a bucket…your bucket can talk. Eyes on a tissue box…your tissue box can talk. Just wiggle the puppet around a bit and it appears to talk, even without a mouth. All it needs are eyes!

BALAAM'S DONKEY

Numbers 22:21-39

Needed:

• Masking tape

Preparation:

• Use a large space for this race.

• **Beforehand**, place a masking tape line near one end of the room as the starting point.

After you tell the story of the donkey who spoke to Balaam from Numbers 22:21-39, run this fun race. You can have as many kids play at a time as you like and have room for. At the signal, the kids will run to the other side of the room, touch the wall, and then turn around and come back. Sounds easy, doesn't it? But, there are two twists to this race.

Preschoolers are *FASCINATED* when you take something they may be used to and add a twist.

Twist 1: The kids must move like a donkey on all fours!

Twist 2: Three times during the race, the leader will shout, "Angel Alert!" The kids must immediately stop and sit back on their heels. The kids will continue when you say, "Ride on!"

Okay, kids, it's time to move and think like a donkey! How does a donkey move? He has four legs, so you need to use your arms and legs to move. In our story, when did the donkey stop? When he saw the angel! Angel alert, angel alert! When you hear that, you have to stop. When did the donkey go on? When the angel was gone. Ride on, ride on. When you hear that, get going, little donkey!

Did you know that you just worked on some major preschool development? Rapid crawling develops those large motor skills and giving the "Angel Alert!" command develops the ability to follow directions. The kids will never know that this race is really good for them!

BEACH BALL DRUM

Psalm 150:3-6 (ICB)

Praise him with trumpet blasts.
Praise him with harps and lyres.
Praise him with tambourines and dancing.
Praise him with stringed instruments and flutes.
Praise him with loud cymbals.
Praise him with crashing cymbals.
Let everything that breathes praise the Lord.
Praise the Lord!

Needed:

- 36" Beach ball
- Small plastic bucket
- Two 12" dowel rods
- Rocks

This beach ball drum is a *FASCINATING* addition to your worship instruments. You'll definitely need more than one though!

Solid color beach balls of all sizes can be ordered inexpensively online.
The photo shows a 36" beach ball, and because it is so oversized, the kids love it even more.

Place a layer of rocks in the bottom of a medium-size bucket. (We spray painted trick or treat buckets black.) Inflate the beach ball as tight as it will go and seal tightly. Place the nozzle into the bucket. You don't want to glue the beach ball to the bucket, because it will periodically need more air.

One kid stands behind each ball with two 12" dowel rod drumsticks. Show them how to pound on the drum, straight down on the top. If they pound on it from the back, the ball will come off the bucket. After a few attempts, they will get the hang of it.

Add this to Christmas worship and stick on some glitter duct tape dots to make the drum look like an upside-down ornament. What a great worship instrument for "Little Drummer Boy"! But, don't limit yourself to Christmas. It's a fun addition to worship anytime.

Read Psalm 150:3-6 slowly and enthusiastically. ***How should you praise God? This scripture sure sounds like God likes to hear all kinds of instruments. You can play instruments loudly and creatively and from your heart. When you do that with praising Him in mind, I think God has a great time listening to you. Let's play our beach ball drums for God!***

BOARDING THE ARK

Genesis 6:1—9:17

Needed:

- Tongue depressors
- Animal cookies
- Bowls

Tell the kids the familiar story of Noah and the Ark…well, it's familiar to you…but consider the fact that they may not have any knowledge of the story outside of seeing a mural with a boat and a bunch of animals. Don't assume. *FASCINATE*. Look through the questions below and make sure you cover all of the story.

Divide the kids into pairs. Each pair will have two tongue depressors and a bowl of animal cookies. At the far end of the room should be an empty bowl for each pair. This bowl is the "ark." Each partner will hold the end of a tongue depressor in one hand. With their free hand, they will then pick out an animal cookie to place on the other end of their tongue depressor. However, the partners must have matching animal cookies—making a pair to carry to the "ark." At the signal, the pair will balance their animal cookies on their tongue depressors and carry them to their team's ark, walking side-by-side. Once the animals have been deposited in the ark (the empty bowl), the players will run back to their starting bowl with the tongue depressors. The first pair to return will get the chance to answer a question about today's story. Here are some sample questions:

- *Why did God want to destroy the earth? (everyone had turned against God)*

- *Who was the only man left who followed God? (Noah)*

- *How many doors did God tell Noah to put on the ark? (one)*

- *How many of each animal did God tell Noah to put in the ark? (two)*

- *Who shut the door of the ark? (God)*

- *How many days did it rain? (40)*

- *What did Noah and his family do when they left the ark? (built an altar)*

- *What did God put in the sky to show He would never again destroy the earth with a flood? (rainbow)*

BREATHING INTO A BOTTLE

2 Kings 4:18-37

Needed:

• Five empty 2-liter bottles

This is so much fun and so simple! You will need five empty 2-liter bottles. Lay these on their sides at one end of the room and position one child by each bottle. Divide all the other kids evenly into five teams and place them at the other end of the room. (Feel free to change the number according to how many kids you have.) Each team is assigned a specific bottle.

Assign one person from each team to stay at the bottle. Their job is to blow into the bottle every time it is stomped on. Demonstrate how this is done by blowing into a bottle no one else is going to use. The first time the kids see this, there eyes will light up and you're sure to see big smiles…because they're *FASCINATED*.

At the signal, one person from each team will run to their bottle and stomp on it, right in the middle across the label, and then return to their team. (Do NOT stomp the length of the bottle, but go across it sideways.) The bottle will collapse under the stomp. The kid stationed at the bottle will bend over and blow into the bottle to reinflate it while the player returns to their team. That player will tag the next team member who will run to the bottle and stomp on it. As soon as the bottle collapses, that team member will return to the team, while the kid stationed at the bottle reinflates it again. Continue doing this until all the kids have had a turn (or as many turns as you like). Make sure that the same kid is reinflating each team's bottle.

That was a lot of work to blow life back into those bottles. When the bottle got flattened, what had to happen to make it back to the way it was supposed to be?

Tell the kids the story of how God used Elisha to breathe life back into a boy from Shunem.

Did anything in this story remind you of us blowing into the bottles? What was the problem in our story? The boy had stopped breathing. He was dead. God told Elisha to do something. What did God tell Elisha to do? Lay on the boy…mouth to mouth. Elisha breathed into the boy, and what happened? He started breathing again! But he did something kind of funny. He sneezed…seven times! Let's pretend sneeze seven times. He was alive! God used Elisha to breathe life back into the boy.

CAN'T TOUCH THIS

2 Corinthians 5:7 (ICB)

We live by what we believe, not by what we can see.

Needed:

- Disposable cups
- Grabbers

For this activity, each team will need a grabber (sometimes referred to as pincher toys). You can get these from any novelty toy site or usually at a party supply store. **Do not show the grabbers to the kids.**

What would you think if I told you I could move these cups without touching them? What would you think if I told you that I think YOU could move them also, without touching them? Hmmm. I don't think so.

Provide each player with a grabber. At the far end of the room place some plastic cups. At the signal, the children with the grabbers will run to the cups, use the grabber to pick up the cup without touching the cup with their hands, and then carry the cup back to the starting line. It is important that they not touch the cup with their hands. Kids are *FASCINATED* with the grabber and are especially proud when they master how to use it.

Were you able to move the cup? Did you touch the cup? You didn't touch the cup, but you still were able to move it. That reminds me of faith. You can't see faith. We can't see God.
Faith is believing that God is with you, even though you can't touch Him.

When you pray, do you believe God is listening? He is! You have faith that God is listening, because you know He's there even though you can't see Him or touch Him.

FASCINATING ACTIVITIES

DISCIPLES IN THE STORM

Matthew 14:22-33

Needed:

- Aluminum foil
- Pennies
- Tub of water

Preparation:

- Cut a 1-foot square piece of aluminum foil for each kid. Everyone will construct his/her own boat made of aluminum foil. The kids will roll of the edges or scrunch up the foil to give the boat some sides.

- Preschoolers are learning about "sink" and "float", and this is a great way to connect that to Bible-learning. The kids will experiment by putting their "boat" in a tub of water to see whose will actually float. Then, make the experience even more fun by adding pennies. See whose will hold the most pennies before it sinks.

Tell the kids the story of when Jesus walked on the water to get to the disciples, and Peter asked to join Him.

Sometimes we have storms in our lives. I'm not talking about the thunderstorms that happen outside your house, but the storms of life. We sometimes call the difficult things in our lives storms. Rainstorms can be scary. It can also be scary when we go through difficult things. Peter found out that it isn't easy to think about the right things during a storm. What happened when he stopped thinking about walking to Jesus and started thinking about how scary the storm was? When Peter started thinking about the big waves and the stormy sky, that's when he got in trouble. That's when he started to sink!

What made our boats sink? We got too many pennies in them! What made Peter start to sink? He had too many scary thoughts in his mind.

Lots of times when we're upset or scared (during the storms in our lives), we can only think about the problem, or we just think about what MIGHT happen. What if this happened? Or what if they do that? We think about the wrong things!

What we need to do is pray and think about how God will take care of us. There's no reason to be scared when you only think about God.

28

DRESS-UP

If you have only one center set up in your preschool room, the dress-up center is definitely the one to have. Your center doesn't have to take up a lot of room. In fact, it can be portable. Use an old trunk, a big suitcase, or a plastic tub to house the costumes and props. The bigger the variety of items in your dress-up center, the more valuable it will be. Most activities have their greatest impact when they're brought out occasionally, but kids *never* tire of dressing up. Having the freedom to become whoever they want is *FASCINATING.*

Dressing up is an excellent way for preschoolers to tell you what they are learning and how they perceive the world around them. They may re-enact the Bible story you've taught them, and you'll recognize what events or names may not quite have been understood the way you thought you presented them. Social skills are exercised as kids create scenarios and conversations that show how they would handle a situation or work out a problem. As you observe, you will notice characteristics and also be able to identify which children have leadership gifts.

Dress-up provides an opportunity for preschoolers to "be" an adult they admire. This is their chance to try out things they perceive they'll do when they "get big."

There is no wrong way to play dress-up. Jump into the conversations and see what you can find out about what your kiddos are thinking. Ask kids to tell you who they want you to be and what part you should play in their dress-up story. And, don't forget to give yourself a silly name. Enter their world and enjoy!

Here are some items to include in your dress-up center, but these are only to whet your creativity juices:

- Hats of all kinds
- Glasses
- Jewelry
- Shepherd headpieces
- Shoes, boots
- Wigs

- Beards, mustaches
- Crown
- Scepter
- Dresses
- Jackets
- Boa

- Shirts
- Vests
- Capes
- Cardboard tubes
- Cardboard boxes

And, make sure you have a full-length mirror at the center.

DROP YOUR NETS...AGAIN!

Luke 5:1-11

Needed:

- Aquarium nets
- Water
- Large containers
- Small containers
- Marbles
- Towels

Divide the kids into groups. Each group will need a small container (like a margarine cup), an aquarium net, 20 marbles, and a large container of water (like the biggest mixing bowl you have, or larger). Place 20 marbles in each container of water.

Set the containers of water on the floor across the room with the net beside each one. You may also want to have some towels handy, because there will be some water mess. The small container will be at the start line where the group is located.

Anytime you give preschoolers something new to use—like the aquarium net—they will be *FASCINATED* by trying to use it. It's like having a new toy!

When the leader shouts, "**Drop your nets in the water!**" the first person from each team will run to their container of water. Each kid will grab their net and try to scoop up ONE marble...only ONE marble. When they have one marble in the net, they take the marble out, leave the net there, and run it back to their team where they will deposit the marble in the small container. Now the next team member can go.

Tell the story from Luke 5:1-11 where Peter's been fishing and hasn't caught anything. Jesus tells him to go out into the deep waters and let down his nets again...and that's when the miracle happens.

When Jesus told Peter to let down the nets for a catch of fish, Peter said that they had been fishing all night and hadn't caught ONE fish. He hadn't caught even one. At least you caught one marble! Yeah!

Then, Peter said that he would obey Jesus and try again. This time, what happened? There were so many fish that Peter had to yell for his friends to bring their boat out to help him. The two boats were so full of fish they thought they might sink! What do you think you would say if you saw that many fish? What would you think about Jesus?

EYE OF A NEEDLE

Matthew 19:16-30

Needed:

- Giant rubber band or smaller rubber bands linked together
- Needle

Preparation:

- A local office supply store will have the giant rubber bands that are used around bundles of documents, magazines, etc. If you can't find one of these big rubber bands, then make your own by knotting a rubber band chain together to make a circle. (See the instructions below.)

- You want the large rubber band or the loop you made to be big enough that a child can stretch it to go through it, but tight enough that it's a difficult task. This will be your eye of the needle.

Choose one child to try to go through the rubber band without any assistance. Start with it over their head and then they will take the rubber band all the way down their body so they can step out of it. This is *FASCINATING* because they've seen rubber bands used before, but never have they tried to get through one. Challenges are *FASCINATING!* If you have multiple rubber bands, then get several kids doing this at the same time. (It's always good to involve as many kids as possible to prevent straying.)

Do you know what the eye of a needle is? It's the hole that you put the thread through.
Is the eye of a needle bigger or smaller than our rubber band? Is a camel bigger or smaller than the person who went through the rubber band?

Hold up a needle and show how small the eye is. *Can you imagine a camel trying to get through this little hole! Whoa! That is a very tiny hole! Jesus was making a point about how difficult—how super hard—it is for rich people to get into heaven. Jesus said that it is easier for a camel to go through the eye of a needle than for a rich man to enter the Kingdom of Heaven. That's going to be pretty hard!*

Does that mean that there are no rich people in heaven? No. Jesus was saying that when people have a lot of things, they get attached to their stuff. They tend to make their stuff more important than anything else—more important than their families, more important than their friends, more important than God. We always need to make sure that God holds the most important place in our lives.

Rubber Band Chain Instructions

- Place two rubber bands end to end, overlapping one rubber band slightly over the end of the other.

- Lift the part of the rubber band that is underneath up, over the part of the rubber band that is on top of it, and then through itself (outside the overlapped part).

- Keep pulling it through and tighten, forming a knot that holds the 2 rubber bands together.

- Repeat this process by adding one rubber band at a time to the chain.

- Tie the ends together to make a loop of your desired size.

FASCINATING READING NOOK

Needed:

- Super big cardboard box
- 100-Bulb string of lights
- Drill

Kids love to have special places to read or play. When they are involved in making this *FASCINATING* reading nook, they'll look for reasons to read…just so they can climb inside!

Find a large cardboard box—big enough for two kids to comfortably fit inside. Set the box on the floor on one of the longer sides. The flaps should be sticking out so the box is open. The side that is against the floor will have no lights on it, because this is the side the kids will sit on when inside the reading nook. Leave the box flaps on, because some kids like to close themselves inside and the flaps make easy "doors."

To make the lit reading nook, drill holes all over the 4 sides of the box that will surround the kids when sitting inside (two ends, top, and back). Look at your string of lights to see how much wire there is between the lights. You don't want the holes too far apart, because your lights won't reach. You'll need to figure out which drill bit works best for your lights. You want the hole to be big enough that the light will poke through (just up to the socket).

The kids will love helping push the lights through the holes as they are drilled (so the light bulbs are on the inside of the box). The socket and all the wiring will be on the outside of the box. Use as many lights as you want. I like to keep the lights plugged in while we're doing this, because they can get a little temperamental when pushing them through the holes. You want to identify any troublemaker bulbs along the way.

Turn out the lights in the room and plug in the reading nook. Find a good book and you're all set for some *FASCINATING* reading adventures!

GLOW STICK PRAYERS

Matthew 5:16 (ICB)

You should be a light for other people. Live so that they will see the good things you do. Live so that they will praise your Father in heaven.

Needed:

- Glow sticks

We are always influencing the people around us by what we do and what we say. "Influencing" means we "show them how." We have the choice to influence them (show them how) to make poor choices, or to influence them (show them how) to make good choices. I want to help people make choices that please God, don't you?

- *How could you influence a friend to make a good choice when they are angry and look like they're going to hit the person they're mad at?* We shine God's light when we make good choices.
- *How could you influence someone on the playground to take turns?* We shine God's light when we make good choices.
- *How could you influence your sister or brother to share the blocks?* We shine God's light when we make good choices.

Pass out a glow stick to each child. Turn off the lights and darken the room as much as possible. No matter how many times a preschooler plays with a glow stick, it always holds a new *FASCINATION. I'm going to be a light for God and help people choose to obey God, so I'm going to bend my glow stick and light it up so everyone around me can see God's light that I am choosing to bring into the world.*

_____ (name of child), *do you want to bring God's light to the world, too? If you do, say "I want to be God's light" and break your glow stick.*

Choose another child and call them by name. Allow time for each child to respond individually.

Encourage the children to experiment with covering up their stick—wrap their hands around it, put it under their pant leg, or stick it in a pocket. *Could you hide your light? Did you still see it glowing? We don't want to hide what we know about God. We want to help the people around us see God!*

Lead the children in a simple prayer asking God to help them be a good influence on their friends and family and even people they don't know who are watching the way they talk and act. *Please, God, help each one of these children* (name them individually) *to help others see You.*

GO IN PAIRS

Luke 10:1-20

Needed:

- Sandwich cookies
- Burlap sacks

Tell the kids the story of how Jesus sent the disciples out in pairs (Luke 10:1-20). You can also use this snack activity to teach working together.

Since the 72 men who followed Jesus were sent out in pairs, the children will pair up for snack time. At the far end of the room, place some sandwich cookies on a table. Form pairs of kids and line them up at one end of the room. The first pair in each line will stand side-by-side and stick their inside legs into a burlap sack, appearing as if they only have three legs. Even though this sounds like the traditional, everybody-knows-this-game, three-legged race, your preschoolers probably haven't experienced it, so they will be *FASCINATED* by trying to work together in this odd way. When the leader yells, "Send them out!" the first pairs will race to the opposite end of the room, where the sandwich cookies are waiting. They will each grab one and return with it. (If you don't have burlap bags, you can loosely tie their legs together with bandanas, strips of old sheeting, or headbands.)

Jesus sent the men out with a partner. You had to go together with a partner to get your snack.

Before you eat your snack, let's look at it. How many cookies are in your sandwich cookie? There are two cookies. What's in between them that holds them together? Icing. Where one cookie goes, the other one goes, too.

When Jesus sent the men out in pairs, what did He want them to do? He wanted them to tell other people about Him. You and your partner both had the same thing to do. What was that? Get to the cookies! The men Jesus sent out all had the same thing to do. They were all supposed to talk about Jesus.

GOD IS CLOSE

Psalm 145:18 (NLT)

The Lord is close to all who call on him, yes, to all who call on him in truth.

Needed:

- Yard stick
- String
- Eye patch
- Large paper clip
- Packing tape

Preparation:

- Cut a piece of string about 7-feet long.
- Tie one end of the string to a large paper clip.
- Tape the other end of the string to the ceiling.
- Adjust the paper clip so that it's about chest level for the children.

The children will take turns standing 4-5 feet away from the paper clip. Cover one eye using an eye patch. Then, they will hold out a yardstick and try to touch the tip of the yardstick to the hanging large paper clip. With only one eye open, it is difficult to make the connection. Remove the patch and try it with both eyes open, and it's easier to judge the distance. It seems pretty simple, but it will totally *FASCINATE* your preschoolers.

This exercise is all about distance and being able to figure out how far away something is. Distance is something preschoolers are busy learning about. ***Which way was it easier for you to touch the paper clip? With the eye patch on or with the eye patch off? What made it easier?***

If your mom is at the grocery store and you're at home, can she help you if you fall down? Why? Because she's too far away. Can your cousins help you learn to ride a bicycle if they live across the country? No. Why? Because they are too far away. Is God ever too far away? God is different. Distance means absolutely nothing to God, because He can be everywhere all the time. God is amazing! He can be with you (point at one child) ***and with you*** (point at another child) ***and with you*** (point at another child)...***all at the same time. We never have to worry about God being too far away.***

Just like we had to take off the eye patch to see clearly where the paper clip was, if we keep our eyes open, we'll see how God is always working and doing miracles in us and all around us. Let's keep our eyes open and watch for what God's doing. That's how we'll always know He's close by...never far away.

GOD MADE THE SUN, MOON, AND STARS

Genesis 1:14 (NLT)

Then God said, "Let lights appear in the sky to separate the day from the night. Let them be signs to mark the seasons, days, and years."

Needed:

- Yellow and white balloons
- Black permanent marker

Preparation:

- Blow up and tie off yellow and white balloons.
- Draw a sun on each of the yellow balloons.
- On white balloons, draw moons and stars.
- Provide enough balloons so that each child has one.

God had separated darkness from the light on Day 1 of creating everything. Darkness was in one place and light was in another. He had separated the waters above from the waters below on Day 2. And on Day 3 of creation, He separated the water from the land and made all kinds of plants. He made big chunks of land where things grew in part of the world and made other places that were covered with water. Earth was a pretty place with the trees and flowers, but God wasn't finished. He had more in mind.

On Day 4, God spoke—He just said the word—and the sun, moon, and stars came to be. When do we see the sun? During the daytime. When do we see the moon? During the nighttime. When do we see the stars? At night. The sun ruled over the day, and the moon and the stars lit up the night. God was pleased with what He had created and said, "This is good." Can you say, "This is good"?

Place all the yellow and white balloons that you have prepared in the center of the room on the floor. At the signal, the kids will pick up a balloon and bat it as high as they can. As they do, they will call out which one it is: sun, moon, or star. Then, they will grab a different balloon, bat it high, and call out what it is. Do this for only 30 seconds, then flash the lights to signal that they should stop. Take a little break and then go at it again! When you're done, put the balloons out of sight, because the kids' *FASCINATION* with them will disrupt anything else you try to do.

GOD SPEAKS TO THE BOY SAMUEL

1 Samuel 3—3:18

In this Bible account, Samuel, who is sleeping, hears his name called three times. Each time Samuel runs into the other room, thinking that Eli has called him. As you tell the story, each time Samuel runs the kids will respond with this rhyme:

"Eli, Eli, what do you want from me?"
"I didn't call you, Samuel. Go back to sleep."

- **Beforehand**, figure out a HEAVY beat to use along with the rhyme. This will utilize the children's music intelligence, and anything set to music moves quickly into long-term memory.

- Before starting the story, go over the rhyme several times in different voices and different volumes. They'll enjoy these variations, and as you are telling the story, they will know the rhyme and be ready when you signal them.

You've prepared to tell a story, but when you use a rhythm and rhyme technique, you invite the kids to become part of the storytelling…and that's *FASCINATING* to them.

Eli was an old Jewish high priest who served the Lord. Samuel was a little boy who lived in the temple with Eli. Eli was Samuel's teacher. Name a teacher you have. Do you live with them? No! But Samuel actually lived with his teacher, Eli.

One of Samuel's jobs was to check the light in the temple. When it was time to go to bed for the night, Samuel checked the light before he fell asleep. Old Eli, whose eyes were becoming so weak that he could barely see, laid down in his usual place. While they were sleeping, the Lord called to little Samuel.

Samuel jumped off his little mat where he was sleeping and ran to Eli and said, "Here I am. You called me?" But Eli said, "I didn't call you. Go back and lie down." Hmmmm. Samuel was sure Eli had called his name.

Signal kids to say the rhyme together.
"Eli, Eli, what do you want from me?"
"I didn't call you, Samuel. Go back to sleep"

So Samuel went back to his bed to lie down. Again the Lord called Samuel. "Samuel! Samuel!"

Signal kids to say the rhyme together.
"Eli, Eli, what do you want from me?"
"I didn't call you, Samuel. Go back to sleep."

Samuel got up again and hurried to Eli. He said, "Here I am. You called me?" But Eli said, "My son, I didn't call. Go back and lie down." I bet Samuel was wondering if Eli was playing a game with him.

Signal kids to say the rhyme together.

"Eli, Eli, what do you want from me?"

"I didn't call you, Samuel. Go back to sleep."

The Lord called Samuel a third time, and Samuel got up and rushed to Eli. He said, "Here I am. You called me!" Then Eli realized that the Lord was calling the boy. So Eli told Samuel, "Go and lie down, and if you hear your name called again, say 'Speak, Lord, for your servant is listening.'" So Samuel said the words over and over to himself, he checked the light, and then went to lie down once again in his place.

Signal kids to say the rhyme together.

"Eli, Eli, what do you want from me?"

"I didn't call you, Samuel. Go back to sleep."

The Lord called again, "Samuel! Samuel!"

Then Samuel almost ran in to Eli, but then he remembered what Eli told him to say: "Speak, for your servant is listening." The Lord spoke to Samuel and told him that God was going to do something great in Israel. That was great news! Samuel was glad to hear that from God. God also said that He was going to punish Eli's sons because they were bad men and didn't respect the Lord. Oh, Samuel wasn't glad to hear that. That was bad news. Samuel was really scared to tell Eli what God had told him.

The next morning, Eli asked Samuel what God had said. Samuel didn't want to tell Eli what he'd heard God say. How would Eli take it? Would Eli be angry with Samuel? After Samuel told Eli everything, Eli said, "He is the Lord. He will do what is right." What do you think you would do if you thought you heard your name in the middle of the night? How do you think you would've felt if God had told you what He told Eli? Do you think Samuel tried to hide from Eli the next morning? Eli was wise and believed that even if it seemed like bad news about his sons, God would do the right thing.

GOD'S LEVEL

2 Timothy 3:16 (ICB)

All Scripture is inspired by God and is useful for teaching and for showing people what is wrong in their lives. It is useful for correcting faults and teaching how to live right.

Needed:

- Levels

Kids are *FASCINATED* by tools…grown-up tools! Show the kids a level. **The bubbles in the level serve a very important purpose. There are two marks on each glass tube.** Make sure everyone can see the two marks on each of the glass tubes in the level. Have as many levels on hand as possible to give lots of hands-on experience. **The direction you hold the level decides which of these marks you use. There's a little bubble inside each glass tube. You're supposed to move the level slightly until the bubble lies right between the two lines. Then, you know whatever you're trying to make level…is level! It's straight and not crooked. It's in the right place when the bubble is exactly between the lines.**

Give each child an opportunity to hold the level against the wall so they think it is straight. Now, show them how to check the bubbles to see if they are accurate. Guide them to move the level ever-so-slightly until the bubbles rest in between the lines.

We can know we are living the way God wants us to, because what we do will line up with what His Word—the Bible—says! The bubble in the level lines up between the lines if what we're working on is level. If what we're doing—our actions—don't line up with God's Word, then we need to change something.

If you think that it might be okay to lie just this one time, you should check with what the Bible says. Does it say that it's okay to lie every once in a while? No. The Word of God—the Bible—is your level, and it says do not lie…period.

What if you started to argue with someone? What does the Bible say? It says in 2 Timothy 2:23 (ICB) to "stay away from foolish and stupid arguments." So, should you argue? No. The Bible is your level, and it says to stay away from arguments.

As you grow up, always check to see what the Bible says so you will line up with how God wants you to live.

HEART FLIP

Ezekiel 11:19 (ICB)

I will give them a desire to respect me completely. I will put a new way to think inside them. I will take out the stubborn heart like stone from their bodies. Then I will give them an obedient heart of flesh.

Needed:

- Toss Across games
- Beanbags
- Red paper hearts
- Clear tape
- Masking tape

Preparation:

- Cut out nine red paper hearts for each Toss Across game and tape each heart to one of the sides of the pieces that flip over.

- These each have three sides, so just choose one of the sides of each triangular flipper.

- The more Toss Across games you can gather, the more kids will get to participate at a time.

What does it mean to have a changed heart? We have a heart inside our chests that pumps blood so that our bodies can live.

- Give the kids time to put their ear to a friend's chest to listen for the heartbeat. This is *FASCINATING* to kids to actually hear what's going on inside their bodies.

And, we have a heart that is the part of us that decides if we want to follow God or not. When someone is willing, God will change their heart that doesn't want to follow Him to a heart that loves Him. God changes hearts from making bad choices to making wise choices. God changes hearts from disobeying Him to wanting to obey Him.

Divide the kids into groups—one group for each game. The games should be positioned where each group can play without crossing over into the playing area of another group. Determine a stand behind line for each game by putting down a piece of masking tape where players stand to toss a beanbag at the game.

Each time players toss a beanbag and success fully turn over one of the pieces so that a heart is exposed, they will yell, "God changes hearts!"

HIGH AND LIFTED UP

Isaiah 6:1 (NKJV)

I saw the Lord sitting on a throne, high and lifted up, and the train of His robe filled the temple.

Supplies:

- Crepe paper streamers
- Paint stir sticks
- Tape

Preparation:

- **Beforehand,** tape some brightly colored crepe paper streamers to one end of two paint stir sticks.
- Now you have two praise sticks.

Ask the kids to volunteer to pray for whatever is on their heart. The first child who is supposed to pray will raise his/her decorated stir sticks high in the air, and all the children will say, "The Lord be high and lifted up!" Then, that child will pray. After the prayer, he/she will pass the praise sticks to the next child who will lift up the sticks. All the children will again say, "The Lord be high and lifted up!" Then, that child will pray. Continue doing this until all children have had an opportunity to pray.

We honor God when we pray. He is high and lifted up by our prayers.

HOLY OF HOLIES

Isaiah 6

Needed:

- Large appliance box
- Craft sticks
- Ballpoint pen
- Container

Preparation:

- For this activity you will need a large appliance box to be the Holy of Holies area of the temple.
- Cut a door flap for children to use to enter and exit the box.
- If you like, drape the box with a large plain tablecloth and add a string of twinkling lights inside.
- Place this box in the middle of the room.

One priest (hold up one finger)...*once a year* (hold up one finger on the other hand) *was chosen to enter the Holy of Holies area of the Temple. This was a super special place. If only one person, once a year, could go in, you know it must've been pretty special. One year, Isaiah (Can you say, Isaiah?) was chosen to go in and there he saw the Lord! Isaiah said that he saw the Lord, high and lifted up. Wow! That must've been mind-blowing! Make a face of how you think Isaiah would've looked. Isaiah was given a special message from God for the people.*

Let's see who is chosen from our group to go into our "Holy of Holies" box this year.

- Write all of the children's names on individual craft sticks using a ballpoint pen.
- Put all of the sticks into a container and draw one out. This child will go into the box for a count of 10 and then come back out.
- When the child comes out, ask him, "What did Isaiah say when he came out of the Holy of Holies?"
- The child should throw his hands in the air and answer, "I saw the Lord high and lifted up!" Being able to enter the Holy of Holies will totally *FASCINATE* your preschoolers!

Well, we'll choose another priest to enter next year. Good thing the year can go by really quickly when you pretend! Happy Easter, Happy 4th of July, Happy Birthday, Happy Thanksgiving, Merry Christmas, Happy New Year! I can't believe another year went by so quickly! Guess it's time to choose a priest to enter the Holy of Holies this year!

- Continue passing through the years and choosing name sticks out of the container to send a new child into the box until all children have had a turn.

I'M GROWING – SERVING OTHERS

Luke 3:11 (ICB)

John answered, "If you have two shirts, share with the person who does not have one. If you have food, share that too."

Needed:

• Clothes that are too small for the kids

Preschoolers are fascinated by doing something that is a "big people" project. So, *FASCINATE* them by giving them an opportunity to serve others, just like big people do.

Preschoolers are very conscious that they are growing. It's such a source of pride when someone says to them, "My, how you have grown since I last saw you," even if that was just a week ago.

Designate a month or quarter when you will use this service project with your group of kids.

What happens to your clothes when you grow a whole bunch? Have you ever tried to put on clothes that fit you last year but are now too small? What would happen if you tried to wear clothes that were way too small? They would rip. Or it wouldn't feel very good.

• Bring out some clothes that are obviously too small for the children.

• Try to put a piece of clothing on each child that is too small.

• It's important that each child participate and experience this for it to have an impact.

The Bible tells us that we should help people who need clothes. You can give away the clothes that you've outgrown, so kids smaller than you will have something to wear. There are special people we can give the clothes to who will give them to kids who need clothing. Let's look in our closets and drawers to see what we have that no longer fits us!

• Communicate the details of the clothing drive to parents.

• Encourage each child to bring in a piece of clothing (that's still in good condition) that they have outgrown.

• You can do this for each week in a month and hang the clothes on a clothesline across the room.

• Determine which week/month will be "pants" week, or "T-shirt" week, or "shoes" week.

JESUS WANTS US TO REMEMBER

John 13:1-17

Needed:

- Wash basin
- Pitcher of water
- Chair
- Long towel

It is important that the kids SEE what happens during foot washing. Some churches have a tradition of a foot washing service. It's a special time when they remember what Jesus did with His disciples and think about their own attitude of serving others. Tell the story found in John 13:1-17 to the children.

Jesus not only ate a special meal with His friends the night before He was taken, but He also did something very special to each of them. He washed their feet! The streets were dusty and people wore sandals. It was the job of a servant to remove the sandals of a guest and wash their feet. The room where Jesus and His disciples shared a meal was a borrowed room, so there was no host, and I guess we could say that they were all guests. So, Jesus got up, put a long towel around His waist, and started washing the feet of each disciple. Jesus was teaching the disciples something about serving others.

- Ask a volunteer ahead of time to allow you to wash her or his feet. Have her remove both shoes and socks and sit in a chair.

- Wrap a long towel around your waist (if you have one of the special foot washing towels); otherwise, have a towel handy.

- Kneel in front of the person with the basin in front of you, at the volunteer's feet.

- Place one foot at a time in a basin of warm water and wash it. Dry her foot with a towel, and then do the same thing with the other foot.

Traditionally, the person kneeling takes this opportunity to tell the person how glad she is to serve her. This can be specific if there has been an incident that has provided you with a special opportunity to serve her. Offer a blessing for the person. This is an intimate time for the two when they can humbly share and serve one another.

Dump the water and refill it to be used again. Now, it's time to let your kids do this. Yes, they can. Please make sure the water is nice and warm. If not, it is a major distraction that will totally ruin this time for preschoolers. (My experience has been that this is a meaningful and memorable experience for preschoolers.) This experience is so unlike anything the kids have ever taken part in that their *FASCINATION* will make it a treasure for life.

What was special about washing your friend's feet?
Why did you like it or not like it?
You don't go around washing other people's feet, but how can you serve them?
How can you do something to make them feel special and loved?

Jesus wanted His disciples to remember that He had served them by washing their feet, especially because He wanted them to remember how important it was to serve others...even after He was gone.

KANGAROO BASKET

Exodus 1:1—2:10

Needed:

- Large sweatshirts with pouch in front
- Small baby dolls
- Baskets

Tell the kids the story of how Jochebed placed her baby boy in a basket and put the basket in the river (Exodus 1:1—2:10). She did this to protect her baby. The princess found the baby, named him Moses, and raised him in the palace.

In this activity, you're going to encourage the kids to act like kangaroos. But first let's learn a little about kangaroos.

A mommy kangaroo has a special place she carries her baby. God made the mommy kangaroo with a pouch in front of her stomach. The baby kangaroo can come out of the pouch, hop around, and then crawl back in when he gets tired. This is how the mommy kangaroo protects her baby. A baby kangaroo has a special name. It's called a joey.

- This would be a great time to find a YouTube video of a mommy kangaroo with her baby. Watching the baby crawl in and out of the pouch is *FASCINATING* (for both kids and adults)!

You will need one big sweatshirt with a pouch, one very small baby doll, and one basket for each group of three kids. One kid from each group will put on a sweatshirt and put a baby doll in the pouch. At the other end of the room, place a basket for each group. At the signal each child with a sweatshirt on will hop like a kangaroo down to his or her basket. They will take their baby doll out of their pouch and say, "Moses' mommy put him in a basket" as they place the doll in the basket.

Moses' mommy did her part to help Moses. Because of her, the baby grew up to be a man of God who led the great nation of Israelites out of slavery.

MEASURE UP

1 Samuel 17:1-54

Needed:

- Painters' tape
- Tape measure
- Marker

Tell the children the story of David slaying Goliath.

- **Beforehand,** place a 9-foot strip of tape up the wall. It's okay if it has to go out onto the ceiling!

This tape will help us understand how tall Goliath was compared to David. The Bible tells us that Goliath was about 9 feet tall. That's how tall this line of tape is! Can you imagine standing next to someone this tall?

- Kids absolutely love to measure and be measured, and it FASCINATES them to see how they are growing!

- Invite each child to come and stand in front of the tape line, marking his height with a line and his initials on the tape so he can see how he measures in comparison.

You are all preschoolers. Do you think David was only 4 or 5 years old? Probably not. The Bible doesn't say exactly how old David was, but what we know about him makes us think that he was probably 12-16 years old when he fought Goliath...not much older than some of your brothers and sisters! David was probably around 5' tall, so let's see where that would be on our line.

- Mark 5' on the wall and see who is closest to that height.

David was taller than you, but still not even close to as tall as Goliath! Do you think David was scared of Goliath? Goliath was much taller and bigger than David. Goliath also had on armor and carried dangerous weapons! David was just a boy who had not been trained and had just a little experience in fighting, because he had killed a lion and a bear while protecting the sheep. But David knew that God was with him! Yeah!

David could've run the opposite direction, but instead he RAN toward the giant...faced him... and David won! David took on the challenge, because he trusted God. David would've said that GOD WON!

MOSES CARRIED THE TABLETS

Exodus 32:15 (ICB)

Then Moses went down the mountain. In his hands he had the two stone tablets with the agreement on them. The commands were written on both sides of each stone, front and back.

Needed:

- Obstacle course
- Paver stones

Preparation:

- Find 1-inch thick paving stones from a local hardware or landscaping store—not the big 2-3 inches thick ones. The thick ones will be too heavy for preschoolers to carry.

- You'll also need to set up an obstacle course that will represent Moses coming down the mountain. Use objects you may already have in the room to help. A table could be a tree branch lying across the path that needs to be crawled under. (Or, if you want to really *FASCINATE* the kids, bring in a tree branch!) Chairs can be large boulders that have to be walked around. (Throw a sheet over them.) A piece of tape on the ground could be a very skinny part of the trail that requires careful balance or use a piece of 2" x 4" beam.

Moses climbed up the mountain and waited while God wrote the 10 Commandments on two stones. When God was finished, Moses couldn't wait to get back down the mountain to share the laws with God's people! But Moses also had to know how important these stones were, especially since they had the rules made out of God's love for His people. He had to be very careful climbing down the mountain, even while hiking around rocks, walking on skinny paths, and ducking under branches.

Paver stones are something new…and *FASCINATING*…to preschoolers.

Have you ever seen stones like this? How about in your yard? These are usually used to decorate around the bushes in someone's yard or around the patio. But today, we're going to pretend they are the stone tablets Moses carried down the mountain—special stones tablets that God had written on.

- Gather the children at the start line for the obstacle course.
- Before the children begin, you'll want to demonstrate the desired movements in and around the course.
- Give the first child a paver stone to carry throughout the course.
- Once he is at least a quarter of the way through, a second child can begin.
- Continue until all children have had an opportunity…or two…or three.

Preschoolers love obstacle courses!

MOSES IN THE BASKET – STORYTELLING

Exodus 1:1—2:10

Needed:

- Blue plastic tablecloth
- Basket without a handle
- Artificial greenery
- String
- Baby doll
- Crown

Preparation:

- **Beforehand,** make a river by cutting a blue plastic tablecloth lengthwise in three strips. Place them end-to-end.

- Put a baby doll in a basket (that doesn't have a handle) and tie a string to it at least the length of the blue plastic "river." It would also be good if the basket had some kind of lid. If you don't have a lid, you can lay a small blanket over the baby.

- Tell the story as below, using the prompts in parentheses.

Creative storytelling *FASCINATES* preschoolers and draws them into the story. Try telling the story of baby Moses in the basket in this way. How did your preschoolers respond?

Pharaoh…that's what they called the king of Egypt…was worried because the number of his slaves—the Israelites—was getting more and more and more. If there were too many of them, then one day they might decide to overthrow him. They might decide that they could take over the king. So, the king came up with an evil, awful, terrible plan. He would get rid of all the little Israelite baby boys. You could hear Israelite mommies and daddies crying all over the country when their little boys were taken away by Pharaoh's soldiers. What a mean king! How sad the mommies and daddies were.

One Israelite mother named Jochebed (Can you say "Jochebed"?), who had a little boy, came up with a plan to save her baby. She would have to work fast, because the baby was getting bigger by the day. Someone would surely hear him cry. Her plan was to make a basket to put the baby in and then float him in the river. Maybe he would float away and someone would find him. Jochebed finished the basket. It was time. She placed the baby boy in the basket. (Put the doll in the basket.)

Jochebed and her daughter, Miriam, walked to the river, carefully carrying the basket where the precious baby boy lay. When they got to the river, Jochebed did a terribly difficult thing. Oh my, this must've been so hard! She said good-bye to her baby boy and placed the basket in the water. She told Miriam to watch from a little ways away. (Place the basket at one end of your blue plastic river. Stretch the string down the plastic to the other end.) *Miriam watched as the basket floated in the water.* (Pull an artificial greenery spray up in front of your face and peek out to the side.)

It wasn't long before some beautifully dressed women came down to the river. It was the princess and her servants! (Put the crown on.) *The princess came to take a bath in the river. Miriam kept watching.* (Put the artificial greenery in front of your face again.) *The princess stopped when she noticed the basket floating in the water. She was so curious. She ordered one of her servants to bring the basket to her.*

(Pull on the string, dragging the basket down the plastic river.) *The princess leaned over the floating basket and removed the lid.* (If your basket has a lid, remove it.) *Oh my! What a surprise! There inside was a wiggling, cooing, little baby boy.*

Immediately, the princess realized this was one of the Israelite babies, but she couldn't resist the little one. She told her servants that she was going to take this baby home and raise him as her own. God placed a wonderful thought in Miriam's head, and she sprang from where she had been watching. (Move the artificial plant aside.) *Miriam told the princess that she knew someone who could care for this little baby until he got old enough to run around the palace. The princess thought that was a brilliant idea and sent Miriam to get this person who could care for the baby. Guess who it was! Miriam went to get Jochebed, the baby's mother, and that's who took care of the baby until he was old enough to join the princess at the palace. Of course, the baby was now protected because he would be an adopted son of the princess. The princess named the baby Moses, because Moses means "drawn out" and he was drawn out of the river.*

Jochebed got to take care of Moses for a few years, and during that time she taught the little boy about the One True God. She wanted him to know about God before going to the palace to live with the princess. The basket had saved Moses' life! From then on, he grew up in the palace like a prince.

The kids will be *FASCINATED* by how you pulled the basket down the river and will want to try it themselves, so allow time for them to experience floating Moses down the river.

What other Bible stories could you use this technique with? Props, action, participation…it all leads to *FASCINATION!*

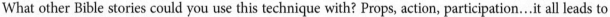

ONE DOOR

Genesis 6:1—9:17

Needed:

- Hula hoop

Tell the children the story of Noah building the ark—the big, big boat—that had only one door.

Hold a hula hoop upright but touching the floor. Explain to the children that this is a door. Each time you give one of the following commands, the kids will do what you say and make that animal sound as they go one at a time through the hula hoop "door."

- Waddle like a duck.
- Gallop like a horse.
- Act like a gorilla.
- Slither like a snake.
- Hop like a frog.
- Fly like an owl.
- Scurry like a mouse.

Encourage the kids to contribute an additional command for everyone to follow.

How many hula hoop doors did we have? We didn't have a whole bunch of hula hoop doors for you to go through. There was only ONE door, and all of the animals you acted like went through that same hula hoop door.

What is a door used for? It's to let someone go from one place to another. How many doors do we have in our room? (You probably have more than one door.) *Where do each one of the doors in our room go to? When the animals all went on the big boat that Noah built, they all went through only ONE door. There was only one door on that big, big boat! It was the only way to get on the boat.*

The story of Noah and the ark is very much about the one door. This door reminds us that there is only one way to God. Jesus is the only way we can know God. Jesus is the only way we can get to heaven. So, Jesus is like a door…and there's only ONE door. We can't believe in anything or anyone else and get to God. There are no other doors…just like there weren't any other doors on the big, big boat.

PAINT CHIP CREATION

Genesis 1:29 (NLT)

Then God said, "Look! I have given you every seed-bearing plant throughout the earth and all the fruit trees for your food."

Needed:

- Paint chip sample strips
- Hole punch
- Gardening/nature magazines

Gather a supply of paint chip sample strips from the paint department of a hardware store. Punch a hole in the paint chip—the bigger the better. You will also need a variety of gardening or nature magazines. Tear out plenty of these pages—don't leave them in the magazine.

On the third day when God was creating everything, He made land. He didn't leave the land full of dirt. No, God had something better in mind. He covered the land with beautiful plants. He made trees, grasses, shrubs, flowers, vines, cacti, fruits, and vegetables to grow on the land. All of the red roses, green apples, orange carrots, purple grapes, yellow squash, and blueberries were made by God! Can you name some more plants God made on Day 3? What's your favorite vegetable? What's your favorite plant? Do you like trees, grass, or flowers best?

Each child will select a colored paint sample. They will flip through the gardening magazine's pictures, finding a plant that matches their paint color. Many may never have seen a paint chip, so they will be FASCINATED to play with them. They will place the paint chip over the page, sliding it around until something of the matching color appears in the punched hole.

End the activity by praying together, *"Thank You, God, for creating the land and all the different plants. We love all the colors You made!"*

- ...unnel
- Pair of sandals

Tell the kids the story of the woman who had been dealing with a health issue for years (Luke 8:42-48). **She knew Jesus could heal her and wanted desperately to just be able to touch the hem of His garment.**

Lay a pair of men's sandals (the more rugged the better) at the end of a play tunnel, about 18" away from the opening—a preschooler's arm's reach. One at a time, the children will crawl through the tunnel. When they get to the opening at the other end of the tunnel, they will stop, and reach out their arm as far as possible to touch a sandal. As they reach for the sandal, encourage them to expressively say, "Jesus, I'm reaching for You!"

Once all the children have done this, have them kneel close enough around the sandals that they can touch them. Pray and thank God for each child. Thank God that we can know that when we reach out for Jesus, He is always there. Changing up the way you conduct prayer time is both a *FASCINATING* and an engaging experience for little ones.

PUMPKIN TOILET PAPER

Psalm 107:1 (ICB)

Thank the Lord because he is good. His love continues forever.

Needed:

- Roll of toilet paper
- 22" Circle of orange material
- Paper grocery sack
- Green chenille stick
- Pencil
- Green fun foam
- Scissors
- Glue dots

Lots of crops are harvested in the fall. Let's name some things that the farmers pick in the fall. How about pumpkins! Have you ever seen a field of pumpkin vines? The orange spots that are pumpkins catch your eye as you look out over all the vines.

Pumpkins remind me of how good God is. I love their bright orange color! Every year God helps all the crops grow so we will have good food to eat. The Bible says that as long as the world exists, God will keep providing food from the ground.

Let's make a special pumpkin. Every time you pass this pumpkin at your house, say, "You are so good, God."

- You will need a 22" circle of lightweight orange material for each pumpkin. It doesn't have to be solid orange, but needs to be something that has a predominantly orange look to it.

- Lay the circle of material so the wrong side is up.

- The children will place a roll of toilet paper in the center of the circle.

- They will pull the edges up around the toilet paper and tuck them into the cardboard roll in the center. It's best to do one tuck from opposite sides as you begin. (Do a north, south, east, and west tuck first.) Keep tucking until all the edges are secured in the cardboard roll. There's no need to glue.

- The child will coil a piece of green chenille stick around a pencil. When they pull it away from the pencil the chenille stick will look like a pumpkin vine. Take one end of this and poke it way down into the center of the toilet paper roll.

- Depending on the children's scissor skills, either they will cut or you can cut out some leaves from green fun foam. Use glue dots to adhere the leaves to the chenille stick.

What an adorable pumpkin! Now everyone say, "You are so good, God!"

SACK MAN

Mark 2:1-12

Needed:

- Paper bags, various sizes
- Balloons
- Staplers
- Permanent markers
- Newspaper
- Paper towel rollers
- Toilet paper rollers
- Packing tape

Tell the kids the wonderful story of the four friends who brought their crippled friend to Jesus and had to cut a hole in the roof of the house to get him in. What a creative group of friends!

- Divide the kids into pairs. They will each make their own paralyzed man, but throughout the process they will need to help each other by holding pieces in place. In addition to making something they can relate to the story, they are building their people skills by working together. Depending on the skills of the age group, you will need to offer assistance, but the kids absolutely love making these paper bag people.

- Provide each group with a blown-up and tied off balloon. The balloon will be the head of the man. The children will give the head facial features by using permanent markers.

Now for the body. The body is made by stuffing a medium-size brown paper bag with newspaper.

- Once the body is sufficiently stuffed, turn down the top of the bag and staple it shut.

- Cut a small slit on each side of the bag where the arms should join the torso.

- The kids will push one paper towel roller through one side and then out the other, to make both arms at once.

- In the bottom of the bag, make 2 small holes for the legs. Make sure these aren't too close to one another or they will rip into each other.

- Poke a toilet paper roller into each hole for the legs.

- Use packing tape to secure the balloon in place as the head of this body.

Once they've completed the man, the kids can pretend to carry him to Jesus, by making a litter/stretcher out of a large towel.

(After I've used this craft, and I visit in homes weeks later, parents tell how their child has played with it like a doll. It's a real winner!)

You can use this guy with lots of different stories, so don't limit yourself to this particular one.

TENT FOR FEAST OF BOOTHS

Nehemiah 8-13

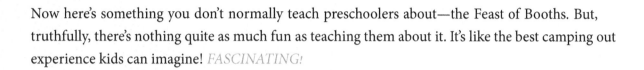

Needed:

- Table
- Chenille sticks
- Small branches of greenery
- Pruners

Now here's something you don't normally teach preschoolers about—the Feast of Booths. But, truthfully, there's nothing quite as much fun as teaching them about it. It's like the best camping out experience kids can imagine! *FASCINATING!*

The Feast of Booths is when the Israelites spent a full week worshipping God. But, they didn't do it from their homes or the temple. They were told to make little huts for their families. This was to help them remember how God had led them for 40 years when they wandered in the desert, waiting to come into the Promised Land. They lived in tents when they were in the desert, and during the Feast of Booths they made tents out of branches and leaves and all kinds of things. The tent was supposed to have a hole in the top, so they could look out at any time and see the heavens that God made.

For those seven days when they were camping in their tent during the Feast of Booths, they praised God, read scriptures, prayed, sang, and had special meals. They celebrated God! Do you think you'd like to stay in a homemade tent for seven days? What would you like about it? Why would you not like it?

The kids will really enjoy making this booth, and it will actually somewhat resemble the booths that families made for the Feast of Booths. (If you're doing this with a larger number of kids, double the tables and greenery supplies.) The kids will cover a tabletop and legs with branches and clippings. They can use chenille sticks (green, brown, black) to attach the greenery to the legs. Without a doubt, they will really get into building their own booth.

When it is completed, seat as many kids as you can inside the booth (under the table) and sing some praise songs. It would also be a great time to read their Bibles together and just thank God for everything He has made.

TRANSPARENCY PUPPETS

Needed:

- Black permanent marker
- Transparency sheet
- Mirror

Kids love puppets! And there are so many ways to create puppets. Here's a way you may not have considered. By using a transparency, YOU can become the puppet.

With a transparency puppet, you can create any look you want for only the cost of a transparency sheet.

- Whoever is going to be the puppet holds the transparency sheet in front of their face and looks into a mirror.
- Use a permanent black marker to put a dot at the inside corner of each eyebrow (over the bridge of your nose).
- Put a dot at each corner of your mouth.
- Depending on what your completed face will look like, you may need to add some additional dots. These are your reference points.

Using the reference dots, draw on eyebrows, glasses, lips, bangs, earrings, or whatever else you want to create your unique puppet.

You can use the transparency puppet to talk with the kids, or you can make one for each of the kids so they can talk with you. Kids who normally will not talk, answer questions, or pray out loud will do so when they have a puppet…even one like this. It breaks down the walls for those who lack self-confidence. If they answer incorrectly, it's not the children answering incorrectly; it's the puppet.

Transparency puppets are tons of fun and will *FASCINATE* your preschoolers!

TRAVELING WITH RUTH

Book of Ruth

Needed:

- Obstacle course (blocks, long piece of 2" x 4")

Preparation:

- Gather items you already have on hand and use them to set up an obstacle course.

- Spread lots of blocks over one area of the floor to show the rocky terrain that Ruth and Naomi would have traveled to get from Moab to Bethlehem.

- The road was also mostly uphill, so if you have access to a ramp, use that…or use a sheet of plywood or 2" x 4" board to create a hill for the kids to walk up. Leave plenty of space between obstacles.

Suggested obstacle course:

- 2" x 4" board—some places were very narrow—walk on the board like a balance beam (or you could put down a piece of masking tape)

- Blocks littering the floor—rocky country—step from one block to the next carefully

- Ramp—walking uphill—take "baby steps" up the ramp

- Sign on the wall for Bethlehem—tap the sign and say, "We're finally here!"

- Tub of water—get across a stream—jump across the tub of water

---

After Naomi's husband died, she wanted to return to Bethlehem to be with the rest of her family. She told the two women, Ruth and Orpah, who had been married to her sons that they could stay behind with their families instead of coming with her. Orpah stayed, but Ruth went with Naomi. Ruth did not want to leave Naomi. Naomi was now her family!

Together Naomi and Ruth traveled from Moab all the way to Bethlehem. The trip would have taken 7-10 days. That's a long way to walk all day long, day after day! The road to Bethlehem was extremely rocky and mostly uphill the whole way. Do you like to walk on rocky ground? How do you feel when you have to walk up a big, big hill? It wasn't an easy trip for Ruth and Naomi!

No matter what, Ruth stayed with Naomi. During the easy parts of the road, Ruth stayed with Naomi. And even during the bad parts, Ruth stayed with Naomi. She didn't turn back.

Lead the children as a group through the first section of the obstacle course. Pause and say, *"This is a really bad part of the road. Should I turn back?"* The children will reply by shouting, "Stay with Naomi!" Once all children have completed the first obstacle, move on to the second. Again, ask if you should return while the children answer, "Stay with Naomi!" Continue in this manner until you have completed the course, and celebrate as you reach "Bethlehem."

WALLS OF JERICHO

Joshua 5:13—6:27

Needed:

- Beach balls

Tell the story from Joshua 5:13—6:27 of how Joshua led the Israelites in their march around the city of Jericho until God caused the walls to fall.

- The kids will link arms to form one long "wall."

- Once the wall is formed, the leaders will throw beach balls at the "wall."

- The kids forming the "wall" will cheer each time a ball is kicked or batted away, but they can only use their heads or feet to bat the ball away…not their hands.

- The "wall" must stay linked together.

- The leaders should throw the beach balls in a way that the ball doesn't make it past the "wall" at any point.

- You're going to hear lots of giggles, and giggles signal that kids are *FASCINATED*!

I bet many armies had tried to knock down the wall before the Israelites arrived. The Israelites knew they couldn't do it alone, so they called on God to help them! What weapons did God tell the Israelites to use? Did they use beach balls? Did they use guns? Did they use arrows? No! They didn't use any of those. They marched and they blew horns and they shouted. The Israelites hung in there and marched around the city of Jericho each day for seven days…just like God told them to. When they blew the horns and shouted, God caused the walls to fall down. What a strange way to make walls fall down! Even though it wasn't what they were used to, the Israelites did exactly as God told them, and because of that, God caused the walls of Jericho to fall down.

- Now, pretend to blow a horn; then everybody shout "Praise God!"
- Instruct the "wall" of kids to fall down!

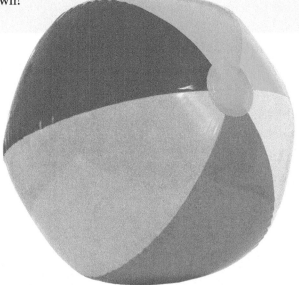

ZIGZAG OR STRAIGHT

Proverbs 4:25 (NLT)

Look straight ahead, and fix your eyes on what lies before you.

Needed:

- Stopwatch
- Traffic cones
- Masking tape

What does it mean to zigzag? What does it mean to go straight? Let's see which one is faster and which one is easier?

- You'll want to do this in a very large room.
- Use the masking tape to create a starting line on one side of the room.
- You will also need a finish line on the other side of the room.
- Between the two lines, set a bunch of traffic cones in an evenly spaced straight line. (The closer they are together, the more zigzagging the children will have to do.)
- Choose one child at a time to race.
- Use the stopwatch to time the child as he runs zigzag around the cones and across the finish line. (You will need to demonstrate before the children begin.)
- Read the time to the group. Then ask the same child to race back to the start line. This time, though, they will just run straight, not using the cones at all. Read this time to the group.
- More than likely, the kids will not be able to tell which is greater, but each time make a statement that they ran faster coming back in a straight line than they did running in a zigzag.

Give each child an opportunity to do the same thing. Continue to show that running in a straight line is faster than zigzagging through the cones.

God wants us to always go straight to Him. When we start making other things more important than God, we get in trouble. It's like we're zigzagging. It's when we don't follow what His Word says that we get in trouble. It's like we're zigzagging. When we lie instead of tell the truth, we're zigzagging. When we say "No" to our parents, we're zigzagging. When you're in a difficult situation and you try to figure it out on your own, you're zigzagging. God wants you to go straight to Him when you're having a difficult time.

How do we go straight to God? We think about Him first. We ask Him for answers. We pray straight to Him. We look straight at His Word, the Bible. No zigzagging!

BARLEY CAKES

Ruth 2:17 (ICB)

So Ruth gathered grain in the field until evening. Then she separated the grain from the chaff. There was about one-half bushel of barley.

Needed:

- Griddle
- Ladle
- Spatula
- Bowl
- Whisk
- Small paper plates

Kids are absolutely *FASCINATED* when they can be involved in cooking! And they learn so much from cooking—measuring, fine motor skills, large motor skills, following directions, not to mention spending personal time with an adult.

Recipe Ingredients

1 c. barley flour	1 ½ c. milk
1 c. flour	pinch salt
2 T. baking powder	1 egg
2 T. sugar	4 T. vegetable oil

It is very likely that Ruth made a cake from the barley she gathered, much like this recipe for pancakes. Instead of vegetable oil she probably used olive oil (so, substitute if you have olive oil available). *We usually eat our pancakes with butter and syrup, but they probably put berries, figs, or meat on them…or just ate them plain. What do you like on your pancakes?*

- Preheat a griddle or large skillet to 350° F.

- Mix all the dry ingredients together that are listed. Every child needs an opportunity to add an ingredient, so other leaders can also make a batch with a group of kids.

- Add in the milk, egg, and oil.

- Stir 50 strokes. (Wait until the flour is incorporated before having the kids help stir…or you'll likely have a crazy mess!) *How far can you count? To 50? Let's see.*

- You want the batter to be thick, but also be able to pour. Add a little more milk if needed to get it to the right consistency.

- Batter may be a little lumpy, but that's okay.

- Use a small ladle to pour batter onto the griddle, leaving space between for ease of turning.

- When the dough dulls and bubbles pop up on top, turn the pancakes to cook on the other side.

What would you think if this was the only food you had to eat? Pancakes for breakfast. Pancakes for lunch. Pancakes for supper. And, how about a pancake as a snack? You might get tired of them. But Ruth was glad that she was able to find grain so they could have something to eat. She was glad to eat pancakes all the time!

CHOCOLATE CHIPS

Philippians 1:3 (NLT)

Every time I think of you, I give thanks to my God.

Needed:

- Bag of melting chocolates
- Bag of ruffle potato chips
- Double boiler
- Rubber spatula
- Waxed paper
- Cookie sheet
- Address labels of Philippians 1:3

Beforehand, print Philippians 1:3 on some address labels. You will need one for each child or for each bag.

- Melt a bag of good melting chocolates in a double boiler. (You could also use a microwave, but heat in 20-30 second increments and stir each time before heating again. It's very easy to burn chocolate when you melt it in a microwave.)

- The kids will go through a bag of ruffle potato chips, picking out the whole ones and gently setting them aside. Use the ruffle type, because they tend to be less likely to break when dipping.

- Cut a piece of waxed paper to cover a cookie sheet. This is what you'll put the chips on when they are ready to cool.

- Show the kids how to hold one end of a potato chip and take it straight down into the chocolate, so the chip is covered about two-thirds of the way.

- Pull it straight up and out of the chocolate. Let it drip over the double boiler until the excess comes off. Do not go in at an angle or come out at an angle. Practice the motion with the kids before actually putting a chip in their hands.

- After the excess has dripped off, place the covered chip on the waxed paper covered cookie sheet.

- Set the tray of chocolate chips in the refrigerator for about 20 minutes to harden the chocolate.

- Apply a pre-made sticker of Philippians 1:3 to the sandwich bag you'll use for packaging, and then fill the bags with chips.

Open your Bible and read Philippians 1:3 to the children. ***Who did you think of when I read this scripture? Is there someone you thank God for every time you think of them? Is there someone you always pray for?*** Lead the children in repeating the scripture in two sections—*"Every time I think of you"* and *"I give thanks to my God."* ***Now, give your bag of chocolate-covered potato chips to the person you are always thankful for.***

EAT BUGS!

Matthew 3:1-12, Mark 1:3-8, Luke 3:1-20, John 1:15-28

Needed:

- Pretzel nuggets
- String
- Tape

Preparation:

- Tie a string around one end of a pretzel stub and tape the other end of the string securely to a door-frame or the ceiling. You'll have to judge how long to cut the string, depending on what you're going to suspend it from and how tall your kids are.
- Hang them at different heights to accommodate the different heights of your kids.

Show the kids the picture of a locust. After you've told the kids about John the Baptist—how he wore itchy clothing made out of camel's hair (scratch, scratch, scratch)…and ate locusts (ewww, yuck, bugs) and wild honey…and lived out in the desert (man, it's hot out here)—enjoy trying to capture this snack. What a fun way to exercise control of all kinds of muscles while problem-solving.

Name something strange you have eaten or seen someone else eat. John ate some strange things out in the wilderness. Do you remember what he ate? Locusts and wild honey. We've got our own locusts that are flying in our room. Personally, I think I like our locusts better than eating the real bugs.

- Each child will need at least one pretzel locust hanging at about their mouth height.
- With hands behind their backs, at the signal they will try to eat their locust pretzel as it's hanging on the string.
- As the children finish swallowing the last of their locust pretzels, they should yell, "John ate bugs!"

AARON'S ROD – EDIBLE PLAY DOUGH

Numbers 17:1-11

Needed:

- Ingredients for the recipe
- Almond slivers
- Parsley sprigs
- Waxed paper

Preparation:

- **Beforehand**, make some edible play dough.
- Mix the flour, cocoa, soda, and salt; set aside.
- In a bowl, cream the margarine with the sugars.
- Mix in the milk and vanilla.
- Gradually blend in the flour mixture. Each batch makes enough for 10-12 rods.
- Store in the refrigerator until you are ready to use the play dough with the kids.

Recipe Ingredients

3 c. flour	1 t. vanilla
½ t. baking soda	2 T. cocoa powder
½ t. salt	½ c. sugar
½ c. softened margarine	¼ c. packed, light brown sugar
¼ c. milk	

After sharing the story of Aaron's rod being the only one that bloomed (from Numbers 17:1-11), do this activity and enjoy the snack.

This play dough will be *FASCINATING*, because the kids won't get in trouble for eating it. Point out, though, that this is a very special play dough. Other play dough that they use at home, at preschool, or at a friend's house is not for eating!

- Give each child a piece of waxed paper and some edible play dough. They will roll their play dough out to make a rod. (The kids will probably refer to this as "making a play dough snake.")

Aaron's rod was different. What happened to Aaron's rod that didn't happen to the others? It was growing leaves and had almonds on it! His rod was alive! What happened to the other rods? Nothing! They were all still dead when Moses went to get them. There were NO leaves on any of the rods, except for the one that belonged to Aaron.

After the kids have made their rod, they can add a few sprigs of fresh parsley and 3 slivers of almond.

- Do this together, showing them first how to add the parsley.
- Once they all have placed their parsley on their Aaron's rod, demonstrate how to add the 3 slivers of almond and then do it together.
- Although eating fresh parsley is supposed to freshen your breath, the children will probably not eat the parsley. It's very inexpensive, though, and will help the children visualize Aaron's unique rod. (Note: Fewer children have an allergy to almonds than any other nut, but you still need to double check.)

IT'S A BURNING BUSH

Exodus 3—4

Needed:

- Pretzel sticks
- Red and yellow food coloring
- Canned white icing
- Paper plate
- Squirt cheese
- Zipper sandwich bags
- Scissors

Preparations:

- Make red and yellow frostings by stirring a few drops of food coloring into some canned icing.
- Put the colored frosting in a zipper sandwich bag.
- Make a TINY snip on one corner of the bag where the frosting will come out.
- Make enough so kids are not waiting long to use them.

The children will create an edible burning bush! Show a complete burning bush beforehand, so the kids know what they're shooting for. Demonstrate how to squirt cheese out of the can and how to use the sandwich bags of frosting. You're doing something they probably haven't done before, so congratulations on *FASCINATING* your preschoolers!

- Each child will form the trunk and sticks of the bush by laying out the pretzel sticks on a paper plate.
- The kids will add six short squirts of cheese or frosting (yellow and red) to the pretzels to represent the flames of the burning bush.

Make sure you use the time while they are making their burning bush snack as a conversation time. This is an opportune time to ask them questions about the story.

Although God's bush did not disappear as it burned, this tasty treat is sure to disappear quickly!

MESSAGE COOKIES

1 Corinthians 1:3 (NLT)

May God our Father and the Lord Jesus Christ give you grace and peace.

Needed:

- Cookie sheet
- Spatula
- Powdered sugar
- Mesh strainer
- Ingredients for cookie dough
- Mixer
- Spatula
- Rolling pin
- Heart cookie cutter
- Plastic wrap
- Letter stencils

This project is in 2 steps. You can do step 1 (making the cookie dough) with the kids, or you can prepare it yourself beforehand.

Recipe Ingredients

1½ c. all-purpose flour

¾ c. cocoa powder

⅛ t. salt

1¼ t. baking powder

¾ c. softened butter

1 egg

1¼ c. sugar

Step 1

Mix the flour, cocoa powder, salt, and baking powder together and set aside. Beat together the butter, sugar, and egg. Slowly add the dry ingredients and incorporate. Wrap in plastic wrap and refrigerate the dough for at least 2 hours before working with it.

Step 2

Now that your dough is chilled, roll it onto a floured surface until it is about 1/8" thick. The kids will press a heart cookie cutter into the dough and gently wiggle it to cut through the dough completely. Help them use a spatula to transfer their cookie to the cookie sheet.

Bake the cookies in a preheated 375° oven for 8-10 minutes. Let them cool for about 5 minutes before trying to remove them from the oven.

Now comes the interesting part. We're going to spell "THANK YOU" and then someone's name on top of the cookies. There will only be one letter on each cookie. Identify for whom the group would like to make these cookies. Who would they like to thank?

You are thankful for this person, but God celebrates them also. He is glad when people help others and do it with a smile. When people follow God, He gives them grace and peace. They enjoy serving others. You are thanking this person because they served—they helped—in some way.

- Put some powdered sugar in a mesh strainer.

- Place a "T" stencil on top of one cookie.

- One child will gently shake the mesh strainer over the stencil that is covering the cookie until the powdered sugar fills the letter.

- Remove the stencil and the powdered sugar letter will show up on the chocolate cookie.

- Continue making each letter until you have spelled out the entire message.

Include every child in delivering the cookies, if at all possible. This connects the preschooler, the project they worked on, and the impact it has on the person they are thanking.

INTRODUCTION TO PAINTING

Preschoolers are *FASCINATED* when they get to experiment with different mediums of painting. There are so many other things to use besides brushes, crayons, and markers. Each time they try a new medium, they exercise new muscles and discover new ways of controlling their bodies.

Get in the habit of including a sticker on every craft. This sticker should give the Scripture reference or tell a caption of how this craft relates to the story the children learned that day. Don't assume that parents automatically know what the connection is. These labels give them wonderful conversation starters and make giving their child positive comments so much easier.

DO NOT limit yourself to the examples we have given in the following pages and use them only for the story cited. There are many ways you can use each one of these mediums and methods!

Consider these as alternate ways of painting:

- Toothbrush
- Feather
- Flyswatter
- Marshmallow
- Marbles
- Hair comb
- Plastic fork
- Scouring brush
- Bubble wrap
- Communion cups
- Flip-flops
- Sliced fruits or vegetables
- Sponges

BATH PUFFS

Genesis 9:12-13 (CEV)

The rainbow that I have put in the sky will be my sign to you and to every living creature on earth. It will remind you that I will keep this promise forever.

Needed:

- Bath puffs
- Styrofoam plates
- Paints of various colors
- Roll of white or light blue paper
- Bucket of soapy water

Kids can make an incredible rainbow to use with the story of Noah by painting with bath puffs.

- Cut large pieces of paper (3 or 4 feet long) from a roll of newsprint or something similar. Each child will need a piece.

- Spread the paint for each color of the rainbow onto a separate Styrofoam plate—red, orange, yellow, green, blue, indigo (dark purple), and (light) purple.

- One bath puff will be assigned to each color of paint and will not be used for any color except for that one.

- The kids will start with the top color red (top of arch). They will dab the bath puff in the red paint and then dab a large arch that goes from the bottom left corner of their paper, up to the center of the top edge, and then comes back down to end in the lower right corner. A leader may need to help with the first one, but once it's in place, all others follow suite and are added under this base arch. The child will leave the red puff with the red paint and move on to the orange paint.

- They will do the same thing with the orange paint, only puff-painting an arch right under and up against the red one they just completed.

- Keep repeating these arches in the rainbow color order until the last color is a small arch in the middle.

AS SOON AS the last child is done with each of the paints, toss the bath puffs into a bucket of soapy water. If you wait at all, the paint will dry in the netting and you will not be able to clean them.

COMMUNION CUPS

Numbers 13:23 (NLT)

When they came to the valley of Eshcol, they cut down a branch with a single cluster of grapes so large that it took two of them to carry it on a pole between them! They also brought back samples of the pomegranates and figs.

Needed:

- Communion cups
- Purple craft paint
- Small disposable plates
- White construction paper
- Cutout paper leaves
- Glue sticks
- Brown marker

Tell the children the story from Numbers 13—14, where the 12 men went to spy on Canaan to find out what it was like.

Moses sent 12 men into Canaan to check it out. He wanted to figure out how to attack them and take over their land. This was the land God had for the Israelites—the Promised Land.

The men came back telling about incredible fruits—how big were the grapes? The bunches of grapes were so huge that it took two men with poles to carry one bunch! Whoa, baby! God had a very special place for the Israelites, not like anything they had ever seen.

On a blank piece of paper, demonstrate how to make a line with a brown marker that will be the stem of the bunch of grapes. The children will make their stems before moving on. This will give them a place to start with their grapes. (You could also do this with a piece of brown construction paper and glue that on.)

Always demonstrate before setting the kids loose when you're using something new to paint with. Hold the bottom of a communion cup and dip the rim in some purple paint that has been spread onto a small plate (thin layer). Then press the rim onto the paper right below the stem to make a purple circle. Continue making these circles until you have a bunch of grapes outlined.

After the grapes are outlined, have the kids use a fresh communion cup, but this time they will hold the rim and dip the bottom in the paint. Fill in the circles they have outlined with the solid circle of paint from the bottom. It won't fill the outlined circle, but that's fine. It adds to the look of the grapes to not have them completely solid.

Finish this wonderful picture by gluing on two grape leaves, previously cut out by the leader.

FLYSWATTER PAINTING

John 21:6 (NLT)

Then he said, "Throw out your net on the right-hand side of the boat, and you'll get some!" So they did, and they couldn't haul in the net because there were so many fish in it.

Needed:

- Flyswatters
- Disposable dinner plates
- Craft paints
- Water
- Plastic garbage bags
- Blue construction paper
- Construction paper fish
- Glue sticks

Preparation:

- **Beforehand**, cut out some fish from various colors of construction paper. You'll want enough for each child to have 4 or 5.

- Prepare the craft paint by watering it down slightly. You don't want it to glob into the flyswatter.

- Right before the children start to paint, spread a very thin layer of paint onto some disposable plates. You can always add more paint if they use it up, but be very sparse with it to begin with.

Oh my! Flyswatter painting is big-time fun! Some of you are thinking there's no way you would set a preschooler loose with a flyswatter and some paint. Your brain is visualizing the creative messes that could possibly be made. Stop, take a breath, and let's talk about it.

- First of all, you want to demonstrate exactly how to do this before bringing out the flyswatters the kids will use.

- Tap the flyswatter gently in a very thin layer of paint that's covering the bottom of a disposable plate.

- Then, carefully move to the paper that you want to paint and gently tap, tap, tap.

- Give very specific instructions and consequences before beginning. If anyone decides to disobey the boundaries, then immediately put the flyswatter in time-out.

- And, of course, you'll want the children sufficiently covered. Cut out a head hole in a large plastic garbage bag and make slits for the arms. This should slip over their heads easily. Then, push up their sleeves tightly.

Tell the children the story from John 21 when Jesus instructs the disciples who had caught nothing to throw their nets over the other side of the boat…and the nets came up so full that they had to be dragged to shore.

Have you ever caught a fish? Have you been with someone who caught a fish? How did you feel when you got the fish in the boat? How do you think the disciples felt when they had fished so long and hadn't caught anything? How do you think they felt when someone yelled at them from the shore and told them they weren't fishing in the right place? Nobody likes to be told how to do something they already know how to do. Then, the disciples realized it was Jesus, and that changed everything! What do you think they did when they saw the nets overflowing with fish?

Give each child a piece of blue construction paper for the water. They will glue on 4 or 5 pre-cut construction paper fish. *These fish are just swimming around in the water, but we need to catch them. We need a net!* Bring out the flyswatters and paint—commence to tapping some fishnet over the top of your fish.

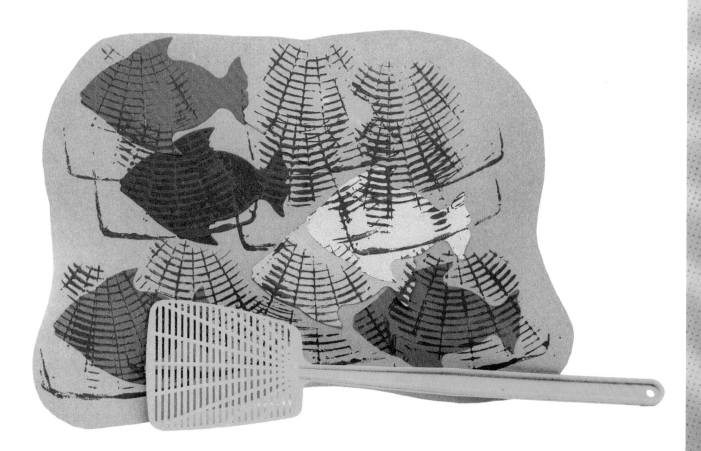

FORK PAINTING

Luke 2:1-20

Needed:

- Light-colored paper
- Address labels
- Plastic forks
- Goldenrod craft paint
- Small paper plates
- Brown/grey paper
- Ice cream test spoons
- Strips of cloth
- Ballpoint pen
- Glue
- Scissors

Post a sample of the completed manger greeting card somewhere in the room where the kids can easily view it. This craft has many steps and uses lots of mediums, and seeing the end product will help kids understand the process.

Give each child a half-sheet of light-colored construction paper. Help them fold it in half to look like a card. On the inside they will place two pre-made labels. The first will need to say "To:" and the second will say "Love: Jesus". Guide them in writing their own name next to the "To:" label. This is something preschoolers are mastering, and this is a wonderful time to exercise this new skill. Don't explain anything else about the craft at this point, until the kids have completed their name writing (or they'll rush through this part). Now close the fold on the construction paper, so the labels are inside.

Cut a rectangle out of brown or gray construction paper about 2"x 3". (Cut these ahead of time.) Glue this piece lengthwise in the center of the folded paper. This will be the main part of the manger. **Let's all do this together.**

Add just a little water to some goldenrod craft paint and then spread a small amount of the watered-down paint on some paper plates. There should just be a **thin film** of paint on each plate. The kids will tap the back of their plastic fork in the paint and then press it against the front of their folded construction paper. (Note: labels are on the inside.) The fork-painted marks will make something that will resemble the straw in the manger, so the kids will put it anywhere they think appropriate for the straw. Set this aside to start drying.

Now it's time to make the baby. Take some strips of cloth that are about ½" wide and wrap those around two-thirds of a wooden ice cream test spoon. Tuck the lose end under some of the wrapping to secure it. (You may want to secure it with some hot glue, but that's only for an adult to use.) The one end of the spoon that isn't covered will be the baby's face. Draw eyes and a mouth on the exposed end with a ballpoint pen. (Markers will bleed into the wood.) Glue the baby in place in the manger that has been drying.

This is a special Christmas card, because it's a card for you! Let the card remind you of what Christmas is all about—God coming TO us as a baby! He came for YOU, and that's why the card is for you. This isn't a card that you give away to someone else. This is a card to keep as if it was sent to you from Jesus. Look at it all this week as you get ready for Christmas.

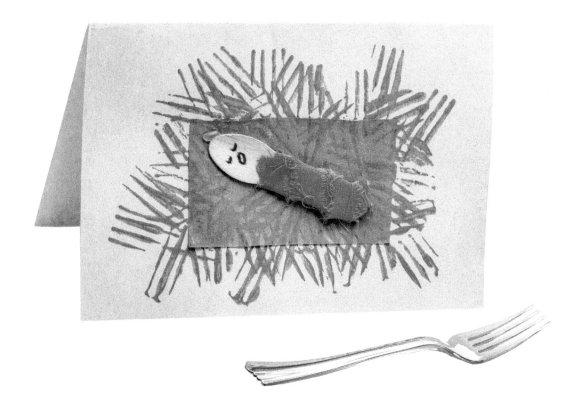

MARBLES

Daniel 3

Needed:

- Marbles
- Condiment cups
- Plastic forks
- Cardboard trays
- Craft paint (red, yellow, orange)
- Bible character cut-outs
- Glue stick
- Crayons
- Manila or white paper
- Tape
- Wet wipes

Preparation:

- Cardboard trays can be found in abundance at grocery stores in the early morning. These are the trays that soup, pop, and cans of vegetables arrive in. They make great carriers for crafts that are still wet when the kids get ready to head home. They also are perfect for marble painting!
- Prepare the craft paint by adding a little water to it. You want it to flow easily and be fairly thin.

Copy the accompanying page for each child. The children will color the three figures—Shadrach, Meshach, and Abednego—with crayons. They should not color in any background. Nothing else…just the three men.

- Then, use one piece of tape at each end to secure the completed coloring paper inside the cardboard tray.

- Squirt some of each watered-down color of paint (red, yellow, orange) in separate condiment cups.

- The children will place a marble in one of the cups and let it get completely covered by the paint.

- They will lift it out of the cup with a plastic fork, letting the excess paint drip off.

- Then, they will place the marble in the corner of their box, and roll it around the box. (There's no need to touch the marble with fingers. It will roll off the fork.) Don't worry about colors getting mixed; it actually adds to the picture.

- Continue doing this with all three colors of craft paint to create the flames that surrounded Shadrach, Meshach, and Abednego.

Keep wet wipes handy to clean paint off of little fingers.

MARSHMALLOW PAINTING

Luke 15:11-32

Needed:

- Regular size marshmallows
- Powdered sugar
- Food coloring
- Small plates
- Large construction paper
- Large pig cut-out
- Glue stick

Preparation

Your paint will be made from powdered sugar, food coloring, and water. We're going to be painting a pig, so make your powdered sugar paint a light pink. Mix a cup of powdered sugar, a couple of drops of red food coloring, and a tablespoon of water in a bowl. Mix. Add additional amounts of water just a few drops at a time. It doesn't take much water to turn powdered sugar into a thin liquid. You'll have to judge how thick you want your paint to be, but be cautious with the amount of liquid you add as you get it to that point.

Marshmallow painting is *FASCINATING*, because this is not what you usually use a marshmallow for.

- Each child will glue a pig cut-out onto a large piece of construction paper.

- Put a small amount of the prepared paint onto plates where the children can easily reach.

- To paint the pig, the children will dip one end of a marshmallow into the paint and then tap or smear the paint onto the pig until it is completely covered.

- Painting is fun, but clean-up is even better! Just pop the "brush" in your mouth and enjoy a snack. There's no rinsing out brushes!

- You can add "mud" to the picture by painting with chocolate pudding. And, it cleans up just as easily as the powdered sugar paint!

When the son ran out of money and his friends took off, he found a job taking care of pigs. As he was feeding the pigs, he realized that even his father's servants had it better than he did at that moment. So, he headed home to offer to work for his father as a servant. What happened when he got home? Was his father mad that he left? Did he tell him to go away? No! He threw a party to welcome him home!

When you decide to follow God, He celebrates just like this dad did when his son came home. The Bible says that all heaven celebrates. Heaven has a party to welcome you back to God! You may do things that don't please God, but you can decide to go back home to Him…and He'll be ready to give you a big hug.

BLOW DRYER FAITH

2 Corinthians 5:7 (NIV)

For we live by faith, not by sight.

Needed:

- Blow dryer
- Ping-pong ball

Usually, when people saw a miracle that Jesus did, seeing the miracle would help them believe in His power. But having faith is when you believe in something you can't see and don't really understand, but you know it's true.

Your faith will keep you going, when you believe in God, even though you can't see Him and don't understand everything about Him. Your faith will give you strength, even though you can't see God and don't understand everything about Him. Your faith will keep you chasing after Jesus, to get to know Him better every day, even though you can't see Him and don't understand everything about Him. Your faith will power your life, even though you can't see God and don't understand everything about Him. Can you say it with me? Faith is believing in God...even though you can't see Him and don't understand everything about Him

This is a *FASCINATING* activity for kids—chasing a ping-pong ball with a blow dryer! The more blow dryers you have, the more fun this is and the more kids you can engage at once. But watch out...you may blow a breaker if you get too many going simultaneously! (Lesson learned from personal experience.) Always test out your experiment before you present it in front of the kids. (Blow dryer power will differ, as well as the size and weight of the ping-pong ball.)

- Each person with a blow dryer will also have a ping-pong ball.

- The kids will set the ball down on something (floor, table, chair) and then move it around using the air from the blow dryer. Don't let the blow dryer touch the ball!

- Now, let's crank this up a notch! Turn a blow dryer on with the nozzle pointed up.

- Then, hold a ping-pong ball in the air flow about an inch from the nozzle.

- Gently, release the ping-pong ball and it will float.

Can you see what's holding the ball in the air? Do you believe the air is keeping the ball floating? Even though you don't see it, or even understand how it works, you believe that it does. That reminds me of faith—you can't see it, but it's there and it has power.

If you have time, the kids can take turns trying to float the ping-pong ball themselves.

Even though we can't actually see faith, it has power to keep us going...to take us closer to God...and to give us strength.

CHANGING DIRECTION

1 Kings 17:7-16

Needed:

- Tall, clear glass
- Water
- White paper
- Thick black marker

Preparation:

- Draw a thick horizontal arrow on a piece of white paper using a wide black marker. The arrow should be 1"-1½" long and have a filled-in arrowhead.
- You'll need a clear glass/vase that is straight up and down.
- Play with how far to position the paper from the glass, so you're aware how the experiment works with your glass.

Before showing the kids this *FASCINATING* experiment, tell them the story of Elijah and the Widow of Zarephath (found in 1 Kings 17:7-16). Here's how the experiment works:

- Hold the piece of paper up next to the empty glass and have the kids point their finger the same direction the arrow is pointing. If they are learning "right" and "left", this experiment would be a good time to work on that skill.

- Fill the glass with water.

- Then, move the paper over behind the glass. The kids (1 or 2 at a time) should look straight through the glass to see the arrow. Ask them to point their finger the same direction the arrow is pointing now. The arrow should actually switch the direction it is pointing. If it was pointing to the left when it was next to the glass, now it will be pointing to the right when it's behind the water-filled glass.

- Pull the paper out from behind the glass and tell the kids to point where the arrow is pointing; then put it back behind the glass. Do this several times.

- Move the arrow back and forth from beside the glass to behind the glass.

When we trust God, things begin to change. The widow knew she didn't have enough food to give some to Elijah too, but she decided to trust that God had sent Elijah to her. And God changed the direction they were going. When we moved the arrow behind the glass full of water, what happened to it? It changed direction! Can you believe it did that? The arrow switched and turned to point the other direction. I didn't even think that would happen! But that's kind of what happens when we trust God and obey Him. God can change our direction.

How many of you expected the arrow to change direction when the water was poured into the glass? I bet the widow didn't expect God to change the direction of her life the day she met Elijah. But God knew what He was doing! And, God already knows how He is going to take care of you too!

Sometimes, we might think one thing is going to happen. But with God, it may not always go the way we thought it would. God may turn the situation around and do something you weren't expecting. Let's keep our eyes open and watch for God working!

DRY ICE BUBBLE

Philippians 4:8 (ICB)

Brothers, continue to think about the things that are good and worthy of praise. Think about the things that are true and honorable and right and pure and beautiful and respected.

Needed:

- Dry ice
- Protective gloves
- Large metal bowl
- Dawn dish soap
- Warm water
- Measuring cup
- Strip of material

There is nothing that will *FASCINATE* kids faster than participating in a science experiment…and this is an amazing one! (Thank you, Bev Hodel, for showing me this!)

- In a large metal bowl, pour 2 cups of warm water.
- Wearing protective gloves, drop some dry ice into the warm water.
- A fog will appear coming out of the bowl.

We have all kinds of thoughts. Some of them are mean thoughts—maybe how we want to get back at someone who hurt us. Some thoughts may be jealous thoughts—how we wish we could be doing what someone else gets to do. Some thoughts might be pouting thoughts—how you try to get your own way. And you have good thoughts, too, mixed in there. But your thoughts are going all over the place, kind of like this fog that is swirling around and going wherever it pleases.

- Paint (with a brush or your finger) some Dawn dishwashing soap around the entire edge of the bowl.
- Soak a 1" wide, long piece of material (a strip from an old T-shirt works well) in the Dawn soap.
- Pull it out of the soap and let the excess drip off.
- Straighten out the piece of material and hold it tautly across the top of the bowl.
- Move it across the top of the bowl and then back the other direction completely.

Look what happens to the fog. Is it going all over the place now? Now it's all contained in this one giant white bubble. The Bible tells us (Philippians 4:8) to keep our thoughts on good and right and pure things. Don't be thinking those other mean, bad thoughts. Keep thinking about Jesus and what He wants you to think about. Round up those good thoughts and keep them, but don't let the bad thoughts in. What does this big bubble look like to you? To me, it looks like a head, a brain. All the thoughts in our brain need to focus on what Jesus wants us to think about.

- *Now, touch the bubble to make it pop. The fog starts going wherever it pleases again.*

If we don't guard our thoughts, they'll go right back to thinking mean, bad things again. Let's keep our thoughts on true, honorable, right, pure things that are worthy of praise.

FASCINATING SAND

Psalm 139:13-14 (ICB)

You made my whole being. You formed me in my mother's body. I praise you because you made me in an amazing and wonderful way. What you have done is wonderful. I know this very well.

Needed:

- Fine, colored sand
- Scotch Guard
- Aluminum foil
- Large cookie sheet
- Condiment bottle
- Clear jar
- Water

Preparation:

- You can make the sand ahead of time if you're using it with a group. If you're going to use it with your kids at home, invite them to help in making it.

- Line a large cookie sheet with aluminum foil.

- Spread a thin layer of colored sand over the entire area of the cookie sheet.

- Spray the sand with Scotch Guard. (I like to do this on the floor of my garage where any overspray won't get on anything except the concrete.)

- Give it a minute to dry, then mix the sand around.

- Spread it out again in the same manner and spray the entire layer with the Scotch Guard again. Let it dry a little bit, mix, spray…repeat this cycle until you've sprayed the sand layer completely 5 times.

Now comes the really *FASCINATING* part. Find an old ketchup or mustard squeeze bottle and fill it with the sand you have prepared. Use a permanent marker to label the bottle so it's not accidentally assumed to have ketchup in it! Yikes, that would be a bad surprise! Fill a large clear jar about two-thirds with water. Put the tip of the condiment bottle down in the water and squeeze. The sand will make incredible designs that will hold their shape underwater. Make your own designs under water.

You made a pretty wonderful design with this special sand! How did it feel to make something out of the sand? Were you excited about what you made? The designs we made with the sand remind me of some words in the Bible that tell us that God designed each of us. He thought about what you would look like, the things you would enjoy, and the things you wouldn't want to eat. What else do you think God decided about you before He made you? I bet He had fun putting you together, even more than the fun we had making our sand creations!

The Bible says God made each one of you wonderful! Let's praise God for designing you the way you are. Let's thank Him for creating you and for thinking you are wonderful.

When you're done, gently pour the water off. Even if you think all the water is off, shake the jar around a bit and some water drops will make their way to the top. The sand will be dry and can be put back in the condiment bottle for reuse once all the water is removed…another *FASCINATING* part of using this sand.

FIZZY COALS

Isaiah 6:6-8

Needed:

- Baking soda
- Water
- Food coloring
- Bowl
- Spoon
- Measuring cups
- Tray
- Vinegar
- Cups
- Wax paper

Preparation:

- This experiment requires some preparation prior to the day when you're going to use it, but believe me, it is so worth it!
- In a bowl, mix together 1 cup baking soda and ¼ cup water.
- You want the dough to be moldable but not so wet it won't form into balls, so you may need to add a little more water or baking soda to adjust.
- Add different colors of food coloring until the dough is black (really dark brown/purple).
- Form the dough into small balls of "coal", about the size of a shooter marble.
- Set them on some wax paper to dry for at least 24 hours.

Tell the kids how God sent an angel to touch Isaiah's lips with burning coals (Isaiah 6:6-8). *Isaiah was super anxious to be sent by God to tell all the people about how awesome God is.*

- With the children, pour cups halfway full of vinegar.
- You will want to use small, clear plastic cups like those typically used when serving punch.
- Give each child a piece of "coal" and a cup.
- Place the cups on a towel or cookie sheet just in case they bubble over.
- The kids will gently drop the coal into the cup and watch it fizz and bubble!

Did you see how much the cup fizzed up inside and bubbled over? All of that happened just because we took our special "coal" and let it touch the vinegar in the cup. This reminds me of what happened to Isaiah. The angel took coal and touched Isaiah's lips, and he got all fizzy inside. He just couldn't help but offer to be the one to be sent out with God's message for the people. Isaiah had seen the Lord high and lifted up when he was in the Holy of Holies, and he was bubbling with excitement to take God's message to the people.

KEEP OUT!

Matthew 6:33 (ICB)

The thing you should want most is God's kingdom and doing what God wants. Then all these other things you need will be given to you.

Needed:

- Pitcher
- Dirty water
- Cheesecloth
- Clear jar
- Heavy rubber band

It's serious business to put something before God! The first two commandments tell us not to make anything more important than God. Anything that we think is more important than God is called an idol. God knows us inside and out—He knows what we look like. And, He knows what we're thinking or if we're in a bad mood. He even knows when you want pancakes for breakfast before you say it out loud! Many people who say they love God have placed idols in front of God—they've made something more important than Him, like their job, the things they own...like toys or clothes or a trampoline, or it could even be their family or a pet. God knows who has put Him first—before anything and everything!

If you start thinking, "My Legos are the most important thing to me," then you've made Legos your idol and they're more important than God. Or if you want to watch a cartoon instead of going to church, then you've made the cartoon an idol. It's more important than worshipping and learning about God. What other things could you make more important than God? All of those things are junk compared to God! We need to keep them out of first place in our hearts.

Are you ready to *FASCINATE* your kids? Here you go!

- Cover the top of a clear jar with cheesecloth, holding it in place with a heavy rubber band.

- Pour some dirty water slowly into the cheesecloth and let it work its way through the material. The dirt will be left behind on the cheesecloth, and the clean water will go on through.

- This is something you should demonstrate first to the kids, but then you should also give them an opportunity to do it themselves and see how the impurities are sifted out.

What happened when we poured the dirty water through the cheesecloth? The dirt stayed behind and the pure water went through. The cheesecloth wouldn't let the other stuff get into the jar with the clean water. It removed it. You need to be like the cheesecloth. Say what?! Yes, you need to be like the cheesecloth! When something tries to take first place away from God, you need to keep it out. You can still enjoy those things, like video games and movies and your Legos. But you have to keep them from becoming the most important thing in your life. The Bible tells us to keep God first and all the other stuff will come along behind God.

KINETIC SAND

Needed:

- 50 lb. Bag of fine sand
- 6 cups of cornstarch
- 6 cups water
- 1 T. Dish soap
- Large storage tub

Commercially made kinetic sand is so expensive for a small amount. For about $10 you can make 50 pounds of kinetic sand and have a *FASCINATING* experience as you do!

- Involve a few kids in helping you prepare the kinetic sand.
- Put 50 pounds of fine sand in a storage tub.
- Pour in 6 cups of cornstarch.
- Thoroughly mix the cornstarch throughout the sand. This will keep little hands busy for a few minutes, and they'll enjoy the texture of the sand.
- Add a tablespoon of dish soap to 6 cups of water.
- Pour this into the sand/cornstarch combination and mix, mix, mix.
- Push up your sleeves and get in there with your hands.

You have just created a medium that will facilitate hours of creative play. The *FASCINATING* thing about kinetic sand is that it keeps its shape easily.

- Pack little bathroom cups with the kinetic sand and build the wall of Jericho.
- Make the well that Joseph's brothers put him in.
- Create a road with rocks and boulders along the sides for the story of the Good Samaritan.

Kinetic sand is a great tool to have on hand for what I call Mosey-In Time. As the kids arrive, they need to immediately engage in an activity that connects them with that day's lesson. Suggest a direction for their kinetic sand play and see what happens!

SWALLOWED UP!

Psalm 5:12 (NLT)

For you bless the godly, O Lord; you surround them with your shield of love.

Needed:

- Neodymium magnet
- White glue
- Water
- Borax
- Metal filings
- Ziplock bag
- Measuring spoons
- 2 cups

When we follow God, He surrounds us with His love. That's what the Bible tells us. That's what God promises us! Do you like to wrap up in a blanket? How does that make you feel? Safe and warm. It's such a good feeling. We should feel safe, warm, and good because we know that God will surround us all the time with His love.

The Bible also says that His love is like a shield that surrounds us. It protects us. How does it do that? When someone says something mean to you, just remember that God loves you…and that's good. His love protects you from their mean words. When someone calls you "dumb," remember that God loves you and He made you. He would never call you dumb, because He loves you too much. He surrounds you with the shield of His love and that protects you.

There are two *FASCINATING* parts to this exercise.
- First, make a slimy goop with the kids. Mix 1 tablespoon of borax with a cup of warm water. Stir and let it set to dissolve.
- In another cup mix ¼ cup water with ¼ cup white glue. Stir well.
- In a ziplock bag, combine ¼ cup of the glue mixture and ¼ cup of the Borax solution. Zip the bag and start mashing it until you feel a glob form.
- Pull the glob from any excess water and continue to mash the glob in your hands. In a minute it becomes like soft Silly Putty. This is so much fun to play with, but let's take it a step further.

Now, for the second *FASCINATING* part.
- Mix ½ teaspoon of metal filings into the goop you've made.
- When it's mixed well, place it on a counter.
- Lay a neodymium magnet on the counter about 2" from the edge of the goop. Be patient and watch the goop move toward the magnet and then, fairly quickly, wrap itself around the magnet completely. ***Where did the magnet go? It's completely wrapped in the goop!***

How does this remind you of what we said about God's love? God wraps you in His love and protects you. He completely surrounds you with His love!

To remove the magnet from the goop is a tedious task. Keep pulling!

INTRODUCTION TO VOCABULARY

It only makes sense that the larger a child's vocabulary, the easier it will be for them to comprehend what they read or hear. The same is true for the Bible. The more of the Bible vocabulary they know and have experienced, the easier it will be for them to comprehend what the Bible says.

It's not unusual for a child by age 6 to have a comprehensive vocabulary of 14,000 words (2010, Cambridge Primary Review Research). Different research projects state that kids 2 to 6 years of age will learn anywhere between 2 and 10 words…wait for it…a day! No matter if it's 2 or 10, that's huge! It's a galloping vocabulary. As adults, we certainly aren't expanding our vocabularies that quickly, no matter how hard we try! Preschoolers seem to possess something I refer to as photographic vocabulary memory. That's not a scientific term. I made it up, but it does describe what I've noticed in preschoolers.

"Photographic vocabulary memory" is my way of describing this wild ability that preschoolers have to hear a new word once and IF they experience a visual to go with it, they remember that word permanently. I'm sure you've found yourself asking, "What did he just say?" These big long words fall out of a preschooler's mouth. If you talk with preschoolers, you'll be *FASCINATED* continually with their vocabulary. They only learn those big long words when they have exposure to them.

So, why do we use baby talk and limit ourselves to small, simple words when teaching preschoolers about the Bible? Stop it! Partner with their vocabulary development and embrace this time when they are learning faster than at any other time in their lives. This is the time to give them the tools of understanding "big Bible words."

Since preschoolers learn when they are *FASCINATED*, let's *FASCINATE* them with activities and experiences that engage them with new vocabulary. Let's give them one more tool for understanding the Scriptures when they start reading on their own. The world is giving them plenty of opportunities to learn new vocabulary. Let's provide opportunities for them to gain vocabulary that will help them get to know the One who created the world.

In the following pages, you'll be shown activities that will help preschoolers experience some pretty big Bible words. After reading through the activities, think about what other vocabulary you could help your kids experience. How can you *FASCINATE* them so they learn new words?

ANOINT

1 Samuel 16:13 (NLT)

So as David stood there among his brothers, Samuel took the flask of olive oil he had brought and anointed David with the oil. And the Spirit of the LORD came powerfully upon David from that day on.

Needed:

- Olive oil
- Small paper drinking cups
- Melon
- Large bowl
- Permanent marker

Show the children a bottle of olive oil. *Have any of you seen a bottle of oil like this? You probably have seen it in your kitchen at home. It is called olive oil. We use this mostly for cooking now, but during Bible times, it was used for many other things. People put it on boo-boos—people boo-boos and sheep boo-boos. They put some on their face to soften their skin, in their lamps to burn for light, in a dish for dipping bread (maybe with some spices), and in their hair. They even used it to make soap or clean their diamonds. And, they used it to anoint kings. What does "anoint" mean?*

- Repeat the word "anoint" several times with the kids so they can now say the word.

Anointing is when oil is poured on someone's head for a special reason. God decided to make David the new king. Anointing was a way to point out that someone had a special job to do for God. David was anointed as king when Samuel poured olive oil on his head. Let's pretend we're Samuel and we're going to anoint David.

Create David by drawing a face on one side of the melon (or a balloon). Place the melon in a large bowl. Pour a small amount of oil into a disposable drinking cup for each child. (Don't prepare these ahead of time or the oil will go through the cup!) Taking turns, the children will pour their oil on David's "head" just as Samuel did in the story. As each one pours, they will say, "Samuel anointed David." Do you think your preschoolers will be *FASCINATED* to anoint this pretend David with oil? Of course, they will! Reinforce the word "anoint" as often as possible during the activity.

CONTAGIOUS

Philippians 2:14 (NIV)

Do everything without grumbling or arguing.

Needed

- Lotion
- 2 Colors of glitter
- 2 Paper plates
- Wet wipes

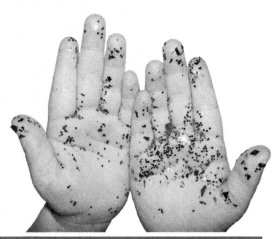

Preparation

- Sprinkle a thin coat of glitter on a paper plate.
- Prepare another plate with a different color of glitter on it.

What does contagious mean? That's a big word! When you have a bad cold, the people around you can catch it, because you're contagious. Contagious means that it's catching. What else is contagious? What can someone "catch" from you? When you think of the good instead of the bad, that attitude is contagious. But grumbling is also contagious!

- Make grumbling noises. Encourage the kids to make the same grumbling sound.
- The leader will rub some lotion on their hands.
- Next, the leader will pat her hands in one color of glitter. The kids will be *FASCINATED* with the glitter, because it's being used in a way that isn't in a craft like they're used to.

This glitter is my good attitude when I'm focused on God and how good He is. That attitude will spread to others around me. It's contagious! "God is good! He is kind. God will be with me through everything."

- While speaking these positive statements, the leader will gently touch the cheeks of several kids.

Look how some of my glitter was left behind on each one I touched. The glitter is my good attitude, and you got some of my attitude on you. When you say nice things and do nice things, other people want to say and do nice things. This shows how my good attitude is contagious.

- Wipe your hands with a wet wipe, dry them thoroughly, and reapply the lotion.
- Dip your hands in the other color of glitter.

Now, this glitter is my grumbling. "This stinks." "Nothing ever goes my way." "I never get chosen first." "But, I want to sit by the teacher." "Rainy days are no fun." Grumble, grumble, grumble.

- While making these bad comments, the leader will touch several children again.

Once again, the glitter is left behind. You see, your bad attitude is contagious, too. It's makes other people start to grumble. When you grumble, it's like spreading glitter all over people, and they've got it on them, too. When you grumble, they join in.

Which way do you think God wants us to be contagious? When we say nice things? Or when we grumble? Name a way you can be contagious this week.

EDAMAME

Luke 15:11-32

Needed:

- Edamame
- Large foil pans
- Mud
- Pan of water
- Paper towels

If you've never eaten edamame, you'll find a bag in the frozen vegetable section, and it is yummy as well as good for you. Maybe you're learning a new word along with the kids! Edamame are baby soybeans in the pod. They are commonly served in Japanese or Chinese restaurants much the same way chips and salsa are served in Mexican restaurants. Before eating, the pods are boiled in water, drained, sprinkled with salt, and then served whole. It's also fun to pop open the pod and eat the beans inside.

- Thaw some edamame and dry them with a paper towel.

- Mix some of the pods in a pan of mud.

- The kids will take turns putting one hand down into the mud to find one edamame.

- Wipe off the muddy hand, and wash off the edamame in the pan of water to give it to the child.

- They can open them and eat the beans, if they like…tasting something new.

- New foods are *FASCINATING* to preschoolers, even if they're not brave enough to actually taste them.

- Encourage the kids to say "edamame" several times. It's a weird word and kind of fun to say.

How would you like to look for your food this way? You'd have to be pretty hungry to do this. In Bible times, the empty bean pods from the carob tree were thrown to the pigs. The pods looked a lot like our edamame pods. Very, very poor people also ate the empty bean pods.

The young man—the Prodigal Son—ran away and spent all of his dad's money. When the money was gone, he found himself feeding pigs the pods from the carob tree. He was so hungry that he wanted to eat the pods himself. Right there in the muddy home of pigs, he decided to run home to his dad. At least he could work for his dad and have food, he thought. But his dad was super happy to see him when he returned. Not only did the son not have to work on his dad's farm, but his dad threw a huge celebration. He even gave his son a ring, a robe, and shoes as gifts!

Let's name our 5 senses. Touch, smell, taste, hear, and see. What senses did you use to learn about edamame? You used your sense of touch to feel down in the mud to find the edamame pod. You used your sense of taste to see if you like the edamame beans. Did you like the edamame? You used your sense of sight to see that the mud was off the edamame.

FLAX

Joshua 1—2

Needed:

- Burlap sample
- Pictures of flax
- Piece of celery

Flax was a plant that was used a lot in Bible times. It has beautiful purple-blue little flowers and grows to be about 3 feet tall.

When the plant was ready to harvest, the entire thing was pulled up; it wasn't cut down like grass. They just yanked it out of the ground, roots and all. Then, it was soaked in water so the plant would pull apart easily.

The women pulled the long stringy fibers away from the stems and then laid the fibers out on the rooftops so they could dry in the sun. Rahab hid the Israelite spies on her rooftop in the drying flax fibers.

- Show the kids a piece of celery and how you can pull the long strings of fiber down the stalk.
- Give them a chance to try pulling the strings of fiber.

Does this look like pieces of thread? This is what the flax was like. Once all the long stringy fibers were dry, they were like thread. The women wove them together to make fabric called linen. That's another new word!

There was rough linen that poor people wore, and it was much like our burlap. Show a sample of burlap and let the kids feel it.

How would you like to wear clothes made out of that? Itchy, itchy! And then, there was fine linen, which the rich people wore that was soft and luxurious. The Bible mentions linen being used in lots of places, including making the curtains for the temple. We still use linen fabric today!

They also used the flax stringy fibers as wicks for their lamps. They lit the fibers, and they burned to give off light. And the oil from the seeds was used to cook with. People today take flax seed oil in a pill or liquid, because it is full of omega-3, which is something that's really good for you.

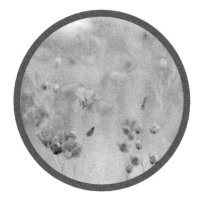  

INCENSE

Psalm 141:2 (NLT)

Accept my prayer as incense offered to you, and my upraised hands as an evening offering.

Needed:

- Lighter
- Empty water bottle or plastic bottle cap
- Disposable foil pan
- Sweet incense

Incense can be found where candles are sold in your discount department store or at a dollar store.

What is a censer? A censer was a tool that only the priests used in the temple. It was a small covered bowl that hung by chains so the priests could carry coals in it from the altar. Imagine the coals you have on a barbeque grill that are very, very hot. They carried the coals in the censer into the sanctuary, where they sprinkled some sweet incense on the coals. Incense is something you burn on purpose, because it smells good when it burns. When the incense started burning against the coals, it sent up a cloud of smoke. Most of the time when something burns, it stinks! But this incense filled the place with a sweet smell, like perfume.

- Put an empty water bottle or a plastic bottle cap in the disposable foil pan and set the flame of the lighter against it so that it begins to melt.
- Let the children smell the burning plastic and describe what they smell. It will be nasty!
- Then, light a little of the incense and let the children smell it.
- Encourage the kids to put into words what the difference is between the smells. Even new smells can be *FASCINATING!*

What would've been the smells of Bible times? There would have been animals everywhere. What do animals, like goats, sheep, and cows, smell like? Stinky! People didn't take a bath every day like we do today. What would the people smell like? Stinky! All kinds of food were prepared over open fires, all at the same time. That could get pretty stinky, too. There were lots of smells that we aren't used to today. The sweet smell of the incense from the censer would've been a nice change from what they usually smelled.

Which direction is the smoke going as it comes off the incense? It's going up, isn't it? The smoke from the incense went up, and the Bible tells us that when we pray, it's like our prayers go up to God, just like the incense smoke. The incense smells sweet and I think when we pray, God thinks it's sweet to hear us talk with Him.

INFLUENCE

Numbers 13–14

Needed:

- Paper clips
- 2 Bar magnets
- Metal cookie sheet
- Permanent marker
- Timer (cell phone)

- With a marker, draw a line across both ends of a cookie sheet about an inch away from the edge.

- Two players will face each other, one at each end of the cookie sheet.

- Scatter 12 paper clips in the center of the cookie sheet.

- Set a timer for one minute.

- An adult will hold the cookie sheet and start the timer.

- Both players will put their magnet under the cookie sheet and begin dragging paper clips to their end of the cookie sheet.

- They can also take paper clips away from their opponent.

- Play is over when the timer goes off.

The word "influence" means that we can "pull" others to think and act the way we do. Our actions and our words can pull or influence other people to see things the way we see them. We can convince other people to be afraid, or worried, or turn down an idea. OR, we can influence…pull…other people to have a good attitude and to be excited about what God is going to do.

Tell the kids the story from Numbers 13—14 about Caleb choosing the land of the giants when Joshua asked him what part of the Promised Land he wanted.

I'm sure when Caleb and Joshua thought about how big those giants were, their knees started shaking a little and they broke out in a sweat. But, they had faith and courage. Caleb and Joshua were excited about going up against the giants because they knew God was with them. They couldn't wait! Joshua influenced Caleb and Caleb influenced Joshua. They got each other excited, instead of getting each other afraid of the giants. You can influence others, too! Are you going to influence others to be afraid, or are you going to influence them to be excited for what God can do?

RAVEN

1 Kings 16:29–17:9

Needed:

- Black feather boa
- Hors d'oeuvre tongs
- Small crackers
- Container of soapy water

A raven is a bird. What color do you think a raven is? It's black…shiny black. How big do you think a raven is? Hold your hands to show me how big you think a raven is. It's about 2 feet long, from head to tail. Show the kids, with your hands, how long 2 feet is. *Can you hold your hands to be 2 feet like a raven? Most people who study birds think the raven is a smart bird. What do you think a raven eats? He eats all kinds of stuff—berries, insects, fruit, and grain. Did you know that ravens are mentioned in the Bible? God used some ravens to take care of a man named Elijah. Let's see what the ravens did.* Show the kids a picture of a raven and give them time to comment.

Tell the kids the story of how Elijah let King Ahab know that there was going to be a drought and a famine. That wasn't good news, and Elijah ran out to the desert because he was afraid of King Ahab. There's no food out in the desert! God provided for Elijah by sending ravens with food and meat every morning and every evening.

The ravens fed Elijah. Let's see if we can pretend to be ravens and deliver food to our friends.

- On yourself, drape a black feather boa from one hand, up the arm, across the shoulders, and down the other arm. Then, use a pair of hors d'oeuvre tongs to pick up a small snack cracker. Instruct one of the kids to tilt their head all the way back and open their mouth wide. Flap your "wings" as you fly across the room to that child, making raven sounds "caw-caw-caw" as you go. Without touching the tongs to the child's mouth, drop the cracker in his or her mouth. As you deliver the cracker, say: *I'm a raven and I'm feeding Elijah.*

The kids will be *FASCINATED* as they each take turns putting on the black feather boa and feeding one of the other children. Make sure they say, "I'm a raven and I'm feeding Elijah." If, by chance, they do touch the mouth of the child they are feeding, have a container of soapy water handy where you can rinse off the tongs.

SCEPTER

Esther 5:2 (ICB)

The king saw Queen Esther standing in the courtyard. When he saw her, he was very pleased. He held out to her the gold scepter that was in his hand. So Esther went up to him and touched the end of the scepter.

Needed:

- Scepter
- Styrofoam ball
- Cardboard paper towel roller
- Gold spray paint

Tell the children the story of Esther becoming queen.

Let's learn a new word today. The word is "scepter." A scepter is a special stick a king holds. No one else holds the scepter, because it's only for the king. When the king points his scepter at you, it means he's calling on you to answer or come to him. If the scepter is pointed at you, it means the king chooses you. In the story of Esther becoming queen, the king pointed his scepter at her to let her know that he had noticed her, and she could come talk with him.

For this "Mother, May I" type game, you will need a scepter. You can make one of these by spray painting a cardboard paper towel roller gold or wrapping the roller in gold wrapping paper. Then, push a large Styrofoam ball down onto one end until the cardboard lodges in the ball securely (about halfway through the ball).

- Choose one child to be the king and stand at one end of the room. The king will need the scepter.

- The other children will line up shoulder-to-shoulder about 20 feet away from the king.

- One at a time, the children will ask the king if they can take a certain number of baby steps, hops, giant steps, or another forward movement by saying, "King, May I take _____."

- The king answers the request in one of two ways. If he is allowing the request, he will point the scepter toward this individual as he replies, "Yes, you may." Otherwise, he will hold the scepter against his chest as he answers, "No, you may not."

- Once the king has given his answer, the next child in line will make her request. After each child has a turn, return to the first child in the line.

- Play continues until one child reaches the king. This child becomes the new king for the next round.

Just like in the game we played, the king used his scepter to allow people to speak to him. If someone wanted to ask the king for something, he could decide to give it to him or not to give it to him. The king had complete control of all of the decisions made for his country and the people who lived there, and whatever he said was what people had to do. If the king said everyone had to eat broccoli, then everyone would have to eat broccoli! Yikes, that made it really important to have a good king and to make sure the king liked you!

THRESH

Judges 6:11-24

Needed:

- Dried wheat
- Cutting board
- Piece of dowel rod (12")

Tell the kids the story of Gideon hiding on the threshing floor. This story will be *FASCINATING* only when the kids understand what "threshing" means. And, oh, how they are going to love experiencing threshing!

Gideon was threshing grain. Does that mean he was picking it? Was he washing it? Was he eating it? I wonder what "threshing" means.

- Hold up a piece of dried grain. (This can be purchased in the dried flower section in a hobby store.)

Here is a piece of wheat. The part that people use to make bread are these little seeds at the ends. We could sit here and pick each one off by hand, and that would take forever, or we could get them off another way. Threshing is how people got the seeds off the stalks of grain in Bible times. (We use machines to do it now.)

They used a special threshing hammer, but I'll show you with this dowel rod. We'll pretend the dowel rod is my threshing hammer.

- Lay the piece of dried wheat on a cutting board.
- Then whack it repeatedly with the piece of dowel rod.
- As you do this, the seeds will separate from the stalk and go flying around the room. Your kids will love seeing you attack the grain!
- But, it gets better! Now it's their turn.
- Give each child some wheat, a cutting board, and a piece of dowel rod.
- As they hit the wheat, encourage them to say, "I'm threshing like Gideon!"

Tidbit

If you question whether or not preschoolers can learn words like "threshing", let me tell you a personal story. I did this exercise with a group of 4-year-olds, which my granddaughter, Kendall, was part of. When I got home, I took all my leftover supplies to the basement, including some of the grain we had used, and placed them on the "I'll-put-this-away-when-I-have-time" table. Several weeks later, Kendall came to visit and we went to the basement to play. She passed the table and noticed the stalks of grain lying there. Very matter-of-factly, she asked, "You been threshing, Grandma?"

UNLEAVENED BREAD

Deuteronomy 16:3 (ICB)

Do not eat it with bread made with yeast. But for seven days eat bread made without yeast. This is the bread of suffering because you left Egypt in a hurry. So all your life you will remember the time you left Egypt.

Needed:

- Matzo crackers
- Packet of yeast
- Small cup
- Spoon
- Lukewarm water

The Passover Feast was a great celebration that helped God's people remember how He saved them from slavery in Egypt—they had been slaves for over 400 years—a really long time! The Israelites worked really, really hard for the Egyptians. They made bricks and built beautiful buildings for the Egyptians. After 400 years of being slaves, God led their escape and showed them the way out of Egypt. The night before they left Egypt, the Israelites prepared their homes. They were in a hurry to leave, so they didn't wait for the bread to rise and get soft and fluffy. They didn't put leavening in it that makes it do that. The leavening is called yeast. It takes hours for bread to rise, and they just couldn't wait around long enough to do that!

Open a packet of yeast and put it in a small cup. Add some lukewarm water and stir. Encourage the kids to smell the yeast. ***Does it smell anything like bread?***

That night the angel "passed over" all the Israelites' homes and kept any of them from being hurt. The Israelites quickly left their homes in Egypt and were free! No more being slaves.

Passover is a very special celebration for God's people. Celebrating Passover was a sign that they were living for God. During Passover they thanked God, and they remembered how God had helped them when they were slaves.

One thing the Israelites always did during the Passover celebration was to eat only unleavened bread— bread that didn't rise. It didn't have the ingredients in it that made it soft and fluffy, so it ended up being like a big cracker. They ate this special type of bread called matzo bread.

- Pass out some matzo crackers and encourage the kids to try them. They may want to sprinkle a little salt on them or even dip them in some honey.

Let's name our five senses—see, hear, taste, smell, and touch. What senses did we use to learn about unleavened bread? Smell…we smelled the yeast, the leaven. Taste…we tasted the matzo cracker, the unleavened bread.

Tidbit

Preschoolers learn through their five senses. Incorporate experiences with their senses any time you can to help them understand new vocabulary.

INTRODUCTION TO SEQUENCING RELAYS

Sequencing relays are a *FASCINATING* way to incorporate math smart (from your multiple intelligences) into retention of Bible stories. Sequencing is an element associated with math. Math isn't just numbers—adding, subtracting, and all that stuff. Through these fun relays, which are all set up basically the same way, kids put the stories in order and exercise their math smart.

Here's how a sequencing relay operates. Choose any story and identify three or four things that happened. For each part of the story, you need to have an action for the kids to do, usually using some kind of a prop. You also need to have a short statement that they make along with the action. It is absolutely necessary for the child to make the statement; otherwise, they will not automatically associate the action with what happened in the story. This is a perfect time to incorporate a youth or older elementary helper to be a prompt at the stations—to help the little ones get this statement out.

Once the child completes the action at Station 1 and says the statement, he or she runs to the next station. They go to Station 2 where they complete the action and say the statement. They continue on in this manner until they complete all stations. That's when they tag the next person who does the same thing. You will find that the kids will listen to the statements as others are running the relay, because they want to do it without assistance from a prompter.

Depending on the size of your space and the number of kids you have, you can set up identical parallel relays. There are no winners. It's just fun to complete it!

After I introduced sequencing relays in workshops, I started hearing back from public school teachers. They shared testimonials of having kids who had difficulty putting things in order, but when they got them involved in sequencing relays, they made huge strides in their retention.

Once you use sequencing relays with your kids, you'll be sold on how beneficial they are. So, come up with some on your own.

CHARIOTS OF FIRE

2 Kings 2:1-18

Needed:

- Masking tape
- Jacket
- Rice
- Small scoop
- 2 Buckets
- Light brown construction paper

This sequencing relay goes along with the story from 2 Kings 2:1-18, where Elisha watches as Elijah is taken away in a chariot of fire.

Set-Up

Station 1: Put down 3 masking tape lines 8"-12" apart and about a foot in length.

Station 2: Place a couple of pieces of light brown construction paper on the floor. This will be the "Muddy Jordan River." Put a rolled up piece of newspaper next to it.

Station 3: Put out a bucket of rice with a small scoop in it and an empty bucket next to it.

Station 4: Lay a vest or coat on the floor.

Running the Sequencing Relay

Station 1: There were 3 places that Elijah told Elisha he was going to go—Bethel, Jericho, and Jordan. The kids will say, "**Elijah went 3 places...1, 2, 3!**" As they count to 3, they will hop from line to line.

Now...run, run, run to the next station!

Station 2: Use the rolled up newspaper to smack the light brown paper. (The Jordan River was muddy.) The kids will say, "**They walked across on dry land.**"

Now...run, run, run to the next station!

Station 3: The kids will use a scoop to move 2 portions of rice from one bucket to the other and say, "**Elisha asked for double.**"

Now...run, run, run to the next station!

Station 4: Put on a jacket or vest and say, "**Elisha put on Elijah's coat.**" Take the jacket off and leave it there before running back to the starting line.

As soon as this round is over, start the next round of children. The children watching can coach the runners if they need help with the phrases they are to say at each station, but MAKE SURE they make the statement at each station.

FOUR FRIENDS TEAR UP A ROOF

Mark 2:1-12

Needed:

- Linoleum tiles
- Hand towels
- Cardboard box
- String
- Gingerbread man cookie cutter

This sequencing relay goes along with the story from Mark 2:1-12, where the four friends bring their crippled friend to Jesus. The only way to get their friend close to Jesus was to dig a hole in the roof and let their friend down.

Set-Up

Station 1: Lay 4 linoleum tiles side-by-side on the floor to make a solid square.

Station 2: Cut a hole in the top of a cardboard box a little bigger than the gingerbread man cookie cutter. Tie a 2-foot piece of string to the cookie cutter and lay it next to the box.

Station 3: Spread a towel out flat on the floor.

Running the Sequencing Relay

Station 1: The child will move the linoleum tiles one at a time to make a similar square right next to the one there. As he moves the tiles, he will say, "**The friends made a hole in the roof!**"

Now...run, run, run to the next station!

Station 2: The child will pick up the end of the string and place it against her forehead. The object is to get the cookie cutter gingerbread man through the hole in the cardboard box. When she does, she will say, "**They let their friend down through the roof!**"

Now...run, run, run to the next station!

Station 3: The kid will start at one end of the towel and roll it up like a jellyroll. When it's completely rolled up, he will throw it over his shoulder and say, "**Pick up your mat and walk!**" Lay down the towel, return to the starting line, and you're done.

You'll need to have parents, older students, or helpers man the stations, so that each time the relay is completed they can put the items back in place (pull the cookie cutter out of the box and lay the towel out flat again).

JOSEPH

Genesis 42

Needed:

- Container of coins
- Crown
- Small scoop
- Bowl
- Corn meal
- Large grocery sack
- Plate
- Crackers

This sequencing relay goes along with the story from Genesis 42, where Joseph is put in charge of storing up grain for the Egyptians. His brothers come to ask for food, and he is able to help them.

Set-Up

Station 1: Provide a container of coins.

Station 2: Set a crown here.

Station 3: At this station there will be a big bowl of corn meal, along with a big sack. Put a small scoop down in the bowl of corn meal.

Station 4: Set out a plate of crackers.

Running the Sequencing Relay

Station 1: Count out 10 coins from the container and stack them. Say: "*Joseph was sold into slavery by his brothers.*"

Now...run, run, run to the next station.

Station 2: Put on a crown. Say: "*Joseph helped the king understand a dream.*"

Now...run, run, run to the next station.

Station 3: Each child will put 2 scoops of corn meal from the bowl into the sack. Once the corn meal has been poured into the sack, he or she will say: "**The king put Joseph in charge of storing up food.**"

Now...run, run, run to the next station.

Station 4: Each child will eat a cracker and rub their stomach. Once the cracker is swallowed, he or she will say, "**Joseph helped his brothers when they needed food.**"

PRAYING FOR PETER

Acts 12:1-16

Needed:

- Large wide rubber bands
- Tinsel loop halo
- Scissors
- Pieces of plywood
- Masking tape

This sequencing relay goes along with the Bible story found in Acts 12:1-16, where an angel lets Peter out of prison. The people who are praying for Peter don't believe it's really him at the door.

Set-Up

Station 1: Place a large wide rubber band for each child.

Station 2: Place a tinsel loop halo and some blunt-end scissors. (The halo is made by taking a piece of tinsel and hot-gluing the ends together.)

Station 3: Place a piece of plywood.

Station 4: Mark an "X" on the floor with some masking tape.

Running the Sequencing Relay

Station 1: Each child will pull a rubber band over his or her feet to resemble the chains around Peter's legs. He or she will then say, "**Peter was in jail.**" Leave the rubber band chains on and hop to the next station.

Now…hop, hop, hop to the next station.

Station 2: The child will pick up the tinsel halo and put it on his head. Then the child will say, "**An angel let Peter out.**" The leader will then use the scissors to cut the child's rubber band chains. Remove the halo and lay it back down before running to next station.

Now…run, run, run to the next station.

Station 3: The child will knock frantically on the wood and say, "**Peter was at the door.**"

Now…run, run, run to the next station.

Station 4: The child will stand on the "X" and jump up and down with her hands over her head. She will say, "**God surprised the people praying!**"

As soon as this round is over, start the next round of children. The children watching can coach the runners if they need help with the phrases they are to say at each station, but MAKE SURE they make the statement at each station.

PRODIGAL SON

Luke 15:11-32

Needed:

- Jar
- Coins
- Socks
- Hula hoop
- Laundry basket
- Pig face image
- Tape
- Beanbags
- Large stuffed animal

Preparation:

- Put some coins inside some long socks and tie them closed.
- Put some coins in a jar.
- Copy the pig face on the next page and tape it to an overturned laundry basket.

Set-Up

Station 1: Place a jar of coins.

Station 2: Set out the socks with coins inside them. Lay down a hula hoop about 4 feet away.

Station 3: Place some beanbags next to the pig laundry basket.

Station 4: Put a large stuffed animal at starting line.

Running the Sequencing Relay

Station 1: The child will reach into the jar and grab a handful of coins while saying, "**Hey, Dad, give me my money**." The child will then empty his handful of coins back into the jar before moving on to the next station.

Now…run, run, run to the next station!

Station 2: The child will pick up one of the sock "moneybags" and toss it into the hula hoop. When he gets it into the hoop, he'll say, "**The son threw away all his money.**"

Now…run, run, run to the next station!

Station 3: The child will "feed the pig" by lifting the laundry basket and putting a bean bag underneath as he says, "**The boy fed pigs.**"

Now…run, run, run to the next station!

Station 4: The child will run all the way back to the starting line and give the large stuffed animal a hug while declaring, "**The dad hugged his son when he came home**."

As soon as this round is over, start the next round of children. The children watching can coach the runners if they need help with the phrases they are to say at each station, but MAKE SURE they make the statement at each station.

SCRIPTURE INDEX

TOPIC INDEX

NOTES

NOTES

CPSIA information can be obtained
at www.ICGtesting.com
Printed in the USA
LVOW05s1932190717
541942LV00005B/6/P